Financial Readiness

Foundational Principles for Stability, Discipline, and Sustainable Money Habits

Adura Gbemi Adegboye

Foreword

Money is one of the most misunderstood forces in human life.

For some, it represents freedom. For others, fear. For many, it is a constant source of pressure, guilt, comparison, or silent worry.

Yet very few people are ever taught how money truly fits into a healthy life. We are taught how to earn.

Sometimes how to spend. Rarely how to *think* clearly about money. Seldom how to build an inner system strong enough to sustain it.

That is why a book like this matters.

This work does not rush the reader into strategies or shortcuts. It begins where real financial change always begins—within the mind, the habits, and the principles that shape everyday decisions. It recognizes a truth often ignored: financial outcomes reflect internal order long before they result from external opportunity.

The pages ahead are not designed to impress you. They are designed to steady you.

They invite you to pause, reflect, and understand the patterns that have quietly influenced your financial life—sometimes for years. They ask thoughtful questions, offer grounded insight, and encourage responsibility without judgment. This is not a book that tells you what to think; it helps you see clearly enough to choose wisely.

What makes this book especially valuable is its balance. It blends wisdom gained from life, psychological insight into human behavior, and practical principles that stand the test of time. It does not separate money from character, discipline, or emotional awareness—because in real life, these things are never separate.

If you are reading this book, you are not late. You are not broken. You are not behind.

You are learning how to build a foundation strong enough to support what is coming next.

Read slowly. Reflect honestly. Apply gently.

This is not about perfection. It is about preparation.

And preparation, done well, changes everything.

INTRODUCTION

This Book Comes Before the Money

Most people believe their financial problems stem from a lack of money. But for many, money is not the first thing missing.

What's missing is understanding. What's missing is preparation. What's missing is a healthy relationship with money itself.

This book was written because too many people are taught how to *chase money* without ever being taught how to hold it, manage it, or live well with it. And when money finally comes—through a job, a business, a breakthrough—it often disappears just as quickly. Not because the person is careless, but because their inner system was never built to sustain it.

If that sounds familiar, let me say this clearly: There is nothing wrong with you. You were not taught what you needed to know.

Financial struggle is rarely just about income. It is about belief, emotion, discipline, fear, confidence, habits, and identity. It is about how you think when money comes—and how you react when it leaves. It is about whether money feels like safety, stress, control, shame, or hope in your hands.

This book is not here to rush you into making money. It is here to help you become ready for money.

Before wealth can grow, there must be order. Before an increase can last, there must be understanding. Before freedom becomes possible, there must be clarity.

In these pages, we will gently examine the invisible forces that shape your financial life—your beliefs, your emotional responses, your habits, and the stories you have carried about money for years, sometimes without realizing it. Not to judge them, but to understand them. Awareness is not about blame; it is about power.

You will not find pressure here. You will not find hype or empty promises. You will not be told that success happens overnight.

Instead, you will be guided—step by step—toward a healthier financial foundation built on wisdom, psychological insight, and practical life principles. The kind of foundation that allows money to stay, grow, and serve your life rather than control it.

Think of this book as preparation. A reset. A quiet rebuilding of your inner financial system.

When you finish this book, you may not yet be richer in numbers—but you will be richer in understanding, calmer in your thinking, and clearer about your next steps. And that is exactly where sustainable financial growth begins.

This is not the end of your financial journey. It is the beginning of doing it the right way.

Take your time. Be honest with yourself. And remember—money responds to clarity long before it responds to effort.

Welcome.

Chapter One

The Real Reason Money Feels Hard

This explanation is written in the same wisdom + psychology + life principles tone you've chosen, and it shows exactly what this chapter is meant to do for the reader, not just what it says.

THE CORE IDEA

Money feels hard, not because people are lazy, unintelligent, or unlucky — but because money activates deep emotional, psychological, and belief-based systems that most people were never taught to understand.

This chapter exists to shift the reader's understanding of their financial struggle from self-blame to self-awareness.

Before a person can learn how to make money, they must first understand:

- Why money feels stressful
- Why money feels confusing
- Why money decisions feel heavy
- Why money never seems to stay

This chapter answers the unspoken question many readers carry: *"Why does money seem so difficult for me, even when I try?"*

WHAT "MONEY FEELS HARD" REALLY MEANS

This chapter clarifies that when people say:

- "Money is hard."
- "Money stresses me."
- "I'm bad with money."
- "Money never lasts."

They rarely talk about numbers. They are talking about:

- Fear
- Pressure
- Confusion
- Emotional exhaustion
- A sense of always being behind

Money feels hard when it is tied to survival, identity, and safety rather than clarity and structure.

WHY MOST PEOPLE MISDIAGNOSE THEIR PROBLEM

Many struggling individuals believe their issue is:

- Not earning enough
- Not being disciplined enough
- Not being smart enough
- Not having the right opportunity

This chapter gently explains that income is often not the first problem. Instead, the deeper issues are:

- A lack of financial understanding
- Emotional reactions to money

- Inherited beliefs about lack and loss
- A nervous system trained for survival, not growth

Until these are addressed, more money often leads to:

- More anxiety
- More impulsive decisions
- More financial leakage
- More self-sabotage

THE PSYCHOLOGICAL SIDE: MONEY AND THE MIND

This chapter introduces the reader to a powerful but simple psychological truth: Money is processed emotionally before it is processed logically.

For many people:

- Money equals safety
- Money equals fear
- Money equals control
- Money equals worth

When money is connected to emotion instead of understanding:

- Decisions become reactive
- Planning feels overwhelming
- Saving feels restrictive

- Earning feels stressful

The chapter explains how:

- Financial stress puts the brain into survival mode
- Survival mode reduces long-term thinking
- Long-term thinking is required for wealth

This helps the reader realize: "I wasn't failing — my mind was protecting me the only way it knew how."

THE ROLE OF UPBRINGING & ENVIRONMENT

Another key concept explained in this chapter is conditioning. Most people learned money by:

- Watching parents struggle
- Hearing phrases like "money doesn't last."
- Growing up around financial instability
- Seeing money cause conflict or stress

Without realizing it, they absorbed beliefs such as:

- "Money disappears"
- "Money causes problems."
- "People like us don't have money."
- "If I get money, I'll lose it."

This chapter helps readers see that many of their money struggles were learned, not chosen. And what is learned can be unlearned.

LIFE PRINCIPLE INTRODUCED IN THIS CHAPTER

Clarity Comes Before Control

This chapter teaches a foundational principle: You cannot control what you do not understand. Trying to control money without understanding it leads to:

- Frustration
- Guilt
- Burnout
- Giving up

But understanding creates:

- Calm
- Awareness
- Better decisions
- Emotional safety

This principle prepares the reader for the rest of the book.

EMOTIONAL HEALING (VERY IMPORTANT)

One of the most important roles of this chapter is emotional release. By the end of Chapter 1, the reader should feel:

- Less shame
- Less self-criticism
- Less pressure to "fix everything now."
- More compassion for themselves

This emotional safety is critical because People cannot learn well while feeling ashamed. This chapter creates a safe mental space for growth.

WHAT THIS CHAPTER IS *NOT* TRYING TO DO

It intentionally does not:

- Teach budgeting
- Teach earning methods
- Push discipline immediately
- Overwhelm the reader with action

Instead, it does something more important: It helps the reader understand their financial struggle without judgment.

HOW THIS CHAPTER PREPARES THE READER FOR THE REST OF THE BOOK

By the end of Chapter 1, the reader:

- Understands that money difficulty has deeper roots
- Stops seeing themselves as "bad with money."
- Becomes open to learning instead of defending
- Is ready to examine beliefs in Chapter 2

This chapter is the emotional and psychological door into the entire series. Without it:

- Readers resist later lessons
- Readers feel attacked or inadequate

- Readers rush and skip foundations

With it:

- Readers stay
- Readers reflect
- Readers grow

The Real Reason Money Feels Hard

For many people, money feels heavy long before it feels practical. It feels stressful before it feels logical. It feels emotional before it ever becomes numerical. This chapter begins by addressing that reality, because until it is understood, no financial strategy—no matter how effective—will truly work.

Most people believe their struggle with money comes from a lack of income. They assume that if they earn more, everything will settle into place. Yet history and experience show that this is often not the case. Many people who experience financial breakthroughs later find themselves back in difficulty, not because they lacked effort or intelligence, but because the internal systems required to handle money were never formed.

Money feels hard when it is tied to survival instead of structure. When cash is associated with fear—fear of running out, fear of not having enough, fear of falling behind—it stops being a neutral tool and becomes an emotional trigger. Every decision then feels urgent. Every expense feels risky. Every opportunity feels overwhelming. In such a state, even small financial choices can feel exhausting.

This chapter gently helps the reader recognize that their financial stress is not a personal weakness. It is often the result of operating in survival mode for too long. Survival mode narrows thinking. It prioritizes immediate relief over long-term stability. When the mind is constantly trying to "get through the month" or "manage the next bill," it has little capacity to plan, build, or grow. This is not failure—it is biology and psychology working exactly as designed.

Money also feels hard because most people were never taught how to understand it beyond earning and spending. As children and young adults, many people learned about money by watching others struggle with it. They heard conversations filled with worry, scarcity, or frustration. They saw money disappear as quickly as it came. Over time, these experiences formed silent beliefs—beliefs that money is unstable, temporary, or difficult to hold onto.

These beliefs often operate beneath awareness. A person may say they want financial freedom, yet unconsciously expect money to leave. They may work hard, yet feel uneasy when they begin to earn more. They may desire stability, yet make decisions that quietly undermine it. This chapter explains that such patterns are not irrational—they are learned responses to past environments.

Another reason money feels hard is that it becomes entangled with identity and self-worth. For many, money is not just a resource; it is a measure of success, responsibility, or failure. When money is scarce, shame often follows. When money is mishandled, guilt takes over. Over time, people begin to associate their financial state with who they are, rather than what they were taught.

This chapter separates the person from the problem. It reinforces a crucial truth: struggling with money does not mean you are irresponsible or incapable—it means you were not prepared. Preparation is not about perfection or expertise; it is about understanding how money interacts with the mind, emotions, habits, and life structure.

One of the most important shifts this chapter introduces is the idea that clarity must come before control. Many people try to control money through restriction, discipline, or force, without ever understanding why their habits exist in the first place. Control without clarity leads to frustration. Clarity, on the other hand, creates calm. When a person understands why they react to money the way they do, they can respond differently.

As the chapter unfolds, the reader is guided to view money as a mirror rather than a judge. Money reflects habits, beliefs, emotional patterns, and life organization. When those underlying elements are disordered, money exposes the disorder. When they are aligned, money flows more smoothly—not magically, but sustainably.

By the end of this chapter, the reader is not expected to have solutions. That is not its purpose. The purpose is awareness. Awareness that financial struggle is often the symptom, not the disease. Awareness that understanding must come before action. Awareness that nothing is "wrong" with them—they are simply standing at the beginning of learning what they were never taught.

This chapter lays the emotional and psychological foundation for the rest of the book. It slows the reader down in a healthy way, removes shame, and creates a sense of safety. Only from this place can real financial growth begin.

The quiet message the reader carries forward is simple but powerful: Money has been hard because understanding came late, not because I am incapable.

And that realization opens the door to everything that follows.

THE CORE MESSAGE THE READER LEAVES WITH

If Chapter 1 does its job well, the reader closes it thinking:

"Money has been hard because I was never taught how to understand it — not because I am incapable."

That single realization is powerful enough to change the entire direction of a person's financial life.

Understanding Financial Struggle Beyond Income

For most people, financial struggle is automatically interpreted as an income problem. When money feels tight, the immediate conclusion is simple: *"I don't earn enough."* This belief is so common that it is often taken for granted. Yet when we look closely at real-life patterns, we begin to see that income alone does not explain why money feels so difficult for so many people.

Some individuals earn modest incomes yet live with relative stability, clarity, and peace. At the same time, others earn significantly more and still feel anxious, overwhelmed, or perpetually behind. This contrast reveals an uncomfortable but important truth: financial struggle is not defined solely by how much money comes in, but by how a person relates to cash, manages it emotionally, and structures their life around it.

When income is treated as the sole solution, deeper issues remain untouched. A person may increase their earnings, only to find that stress increases alongside it. More money can bring bigger decisions, greater pressure, and heightened fear of loss. Without the inner capacity to handle money calmly and intentionally, increased income often magnifies existing problems rather than solving them.

One reason financial struggle persists beyond income is the absence of economic understanding. Many people were never taught how money actually functions in daily life—how to plan with it, pace spending, prepare for irregular expenses, or think beyond immediate needs. As a result, money feels unpredictable. When money feels unpredictable, it feels unsafe. And when something feels unsafe, the mind responds with anxiety and urgency rather than clarity.

Another layer of struggle lies in emotional responses to money. For someone who has experienced lack, money often carries emotional weight. It becomes tied to fear, relief, guilt, or even self-worth. In this state, money is no longer just a tool—it becomes an emotional trigger. Decisions made under emotional pressure tend to be reactive rather than thoughtful, leading to cycles of short-term relief followed by long-term difficulty.

Financial struggle is also deeply connected to habits formed over time. Habits develop quietly, often as coping mechanisms. A person may overspend not because they are careless, but because spending offers temporary comfort or a sense of control. Another may avoid looking at their finances entirely, not out of irresponsibility, but because confronting the numbers brings discomfort or shame. These habits persist regardless of income level unless they are understood and addressed.

Life structure plays an equally important role. When a person's life lacks order—irregular routines, unmanaged obligations, unclear priorities—money reflects that disorder. Expenses appear unexpectedly. Financial decisions are made late or under pressure. There is little room for planning because life itself feels chaotic. In such cases, increasing income without addressing structure is like pouring water into a leaking container.

There is also the influence of belief systems shaped by upbringing and environment. Many people grew up observing financial stress, conflict, or instability. Over time, they internalized the idea that money is temporary, difficult to obtain, or always slipping away. Even when opportunities arise, these beliefs quietly influence behavior, often leading to decisions that confirm the original expectation of struggle.

Understanding financial struggle beyond income means recognizing that money problems are often symptoms, not the root issue. The root lies in awareness, emotional regulation, habits, beliefs, and life organization. Until these elements are examined, financial stress tends to repeat itself in different forms, regardless of how much money is earned.

This perspective is not meant to dismiss the reality of low income or economic hardship. Income does matter. But income alone is not enough. Without understanding, preparation, and internal stability, money cannot function as a source of freedom. It remains a source of tension.

When a person begins to see financial struggle in this broader context, something important happens. Shame begins to lift. The narrative shifts from *"I am bad with money"* to *"I was never shown how to relate to money healthily."* That shift creates space for learning, growth, and change.

This understanding is foundational because it reframes the journey ahead. It tells the reader that before chasing more money, they must first build clarity, stability, and readiness. Only then can income truly serve their life rather than control it.

In essence, to understand financial struggle beyond income is to see money not as the problem itself, but as a reflection of deeper systems within the mind and life. When those systems are strengthened, money becomes easier—not because it magically increases, but because it finally has a stable place to land.

Why Financial Lack Is Not a Personal Failure

One of the most damaging ideas many people carry about money is the belief that financial struggle is proof of personal failure. Over time, this belief settles quietly into the mind, shaping how people see themselves. When money is tight, they do not simply think, *"I'm struggling financially."* They think, *"Something is wrong with me."*

This conclusion feels logical on the surface, especially in a world that constantly celebrates success stories while hiding the complexity behind them. Society often equates financial stability with intelligence, discipline, or worthiness, and financial lack with laziness, irresponsibility, or poor choices. But this narrative is incomplete—and deeply unfair.

Financial lack is not a moral verdict. It is not a measure of intelligence, effort, or value as a human being. In most cases, it is the result of circumstances, conditioning, missing knowledge, and unexamined systems, not personal deficiency.

Many people begin life without access to financial education. They are never taught how money works, how to plan for irregular expenses, how to pace spending, or how to think long-term. Instead, they learn money through observation—watching parents struggle, hearing constant worry, or seeing income disappear under pressure. These early experiences shape expectations long before conscious choices are ever made.

When a person grows up in an environment where money is unstable, the nervous system adapts to survive uncertainty. Decisions become short-term. Relief becomes more important than strategy. This is not failure; it is adaptation. The mind learns to focus on getting through today because tomorrow feels uncertain. Later in life, when stability is required, these survival patterns remain—often misunderstood as irresponsibility.

Financial lack is also strongly influenced by emotional weight. Money is rarely neutral. It becomes connected to fear, shame, responsibility, comparison, and self-worth. A person under financial pressure may make choices that appear irrational from the outside, but internally, those choices often provide momentary relief from stress or anxiety. Again, this is not a lack of character—it is an attempt to cope.

Another reason financial lack is misinterpreted as personal failure is the absence of context. People rarely see the full picture of someone else's monetary journey. They see outcomes without seeing the starting point. They see results without seeing the support systems, timing, opportunities, or safety nets involved. When they compare themselves to these partial images, they assume they alone are falling short.

Life circumstances also play a powerful role. Health challenges, family responsibilities, unstable employment, economic shifts, and unexpected crises all shape financial outcomes. These factors are rarely within a person's full control. Yet many still internalize the impact as if it were entirely their fault.

Perhaps most importantly, financial lack is often the result of misalignment, not incapability. A person may work hard, but in systems that do not fairly reward their effort. They may have skills that were never recognized or nurtured. They may carry beliefs that quietly limit how they earn, save, or take opportunities. None of these reflects personal failure—they reflect misalignment between effort, understanding, and environment.

When financial lack is viewed as personal failure, it creates shame. Shame closes the mind. It discourages learning. It keeps people stuck in cycles of self-criticism rather than growth. But when financial lack is understood as a signal—a message pointing to areas that need clarity, structure, or healing—it becomes informative rather than condemning.

This shift in understanding is powerful. It allows a person to move from self-judgment to self-responsibility. Responsibility does not mean blame; it means recognizing where change is possible. It means saying, *"I was not prepared in this area, but I can learn."* That mindset opens the door to progress.

Recognizing that financial lack is not a personal failure does not remove accountability. Instead, it places responsibility where it belongs—on learning, awareness, and intentional growth rather than self-punishment. It frees the reader to approach money with curiosity rather than fear, and with patience rather than pressure.

At its core, this concept restores dignity. It reminds the reader that struggling financially does not diminish their worth, intelligence, or potential. It simply means they are standing at the beginning of understanding something that was never properly explained to them before.

And understanding, once it begins, changes everything.

The Hidden Mental and Emotional Roots of Money Problems

Money problems rarely begin with money itself. They start quietly, beneath the surface, in the mind and emotions long before they ever appear in bank balances, debts, or unpaid bills. This is why two people with similar incomes can experience completely different financial realities. One may feel calm and in control, while the other feels constantly anxious and overwhelmed. The difference is not intelligence or effort—it is what is happening internally.

At the mental level, money is shaped by belief. Every person carries an internal story about money, whether they are aware of it or not. This story answers questions like: *Is money safe? Is it temporary? Is it hard to keep? Do I deserve it?* These beliefs are rarely formed through conscious thought. They are absorbed through experience—what we observed growing up, what we heard repeatedly, and what we lived through during times of lack or instability.

When a person grows up seeing money disappear quickly, hearing constant worry, or watching conflict arise around finances, the mind learns to associate money with stress and uncertainty. Over time, this creates an expectation of loss. Even when money comes in, the subconscious mind remains alert, waiting for it to leave. This expectation influences decisions in subtle but powerful ways—spending quickly, avoiding planning, or feeling uneasy about saving. These behaviors are often misunderstood as carelessness, when in reality they are protective responses shaped by experience.

Emotionally, money is tied to safety. For many people, money represents security, survival, and stability. When finances are unstable, the nervous system reacts as though there is a threat. This reaction is not logical—it is biological. The body enters a state of alertness, narrowing focus to immediate concerns. Long-term thinking becomes difficult. Planning feels overwhelming. In this state, even good financial advice can feel inaccessible, not because it is wrong, but because the mind is too busy trying to feel safe.

Fear plays a significant role here. Fear of running out. Fear of not being enough. Fear of making the wrong decision. These fears often operate silently, shaping behavior without being named. A person may avoid looking at their finances because it triggers anxiety. Another may overspend to feel relief or a sense of control, even briefly. These actions are not rooted in ignorance—they are rooted in emotional regulation.

Shame is another powerful emotional root of money problems. When financial struggles are internalized as personal failure, they can lead to embarrassment and self-judgment. Shame causes people to hide—not just from others, but from their own reality. Bills go unopened. Numbers go unchecked. Conversations are avoided. The problem grows not because the person does not care, but because shame makes it painful to engage.

There is also the emotional weight of comparison. In a world where success is constantly displayed, many people measure their financial life against incomplete images of others. This comparison quietly erodes confidence. It creates the feeling of always being behind, always late, always lacking. From this emotional position, decisions are often rushed or reactive, driven by the desire to "catch up" rather than build steadily.

Mental exhaustion adds another layer. Financial stress consumes mental energy. When the mind is constantly calculating, worrying, or anticipating problems, it becomes fatigued. Fatigue reduces patience and clarity. Under mental strain, people are more likely to choose short-term relief over long-term benefit. Again, this is not a character flaw—it is the mind responding to overload.

Another hidden root lies in identity. Some people unconsciously define themselves as "bad with money," "not a financial person," or "someone who never has enough." These identities become self-fulfilling. When a person believes money competence is not part of who they are, they approach financial decisions with doubt and hesitation. Over time, this doubt reinforces the original belief.

All of these mental and emotional roots operate quietly. They do not announce themselves. They shape patterns, habits, and reactions over the years. And because they are hidden, people often try to fix money problems at the surface—earning more, cutting expenses, forcing discipline—without addressing what is driving their behavior beneath the surface.

Understanding these roots changes the entire conversation around money. It shifts the focus from blame to awareness. It allows a person to see their financial patterns not as proof of failure, but as signals pointing to unmet needs, unresolved fear, or learned responses that no longer serve them.

This awareness is not meant to excuse poor decisions, but to explain them. Explanation creates space for change. When a person understands *why* they struggle, they regain choice. They can respond instead of react. They can build systems that support their emotional reality rather than fight against it.

At its core, addressing the hidden mental and emotional roots of money problems is about restoring safety and clarity. When the mind feels safe, it can plan. When emotions are acknowledged, they lose control. And when understanding replaces shame, money begins to feel less heavy—not because circumstances change overnight, but because the internal struggle softens.

This is why real financial healing begins inside. Numbers matter, but the mind decides how to handle them. Until the inner roots are understood, money problems tend to repeat themselves in different forms. Once they are understood, change becomes possible—and sustainable.

How Fear, Pressure, and Confusion Distort Financial Decisions

Financial decisions are rarely made in calm conditions. For many people, money decisions are made while the mind is tense, the body is tired, and emotions are already overwhelmed. Fear, pressure, and confusion often sit quietly in the background, shaping choices long before logic has a chance to speak. Understanding how these forces operate is essential because they do not just influence money decisions—they quietly control them.

Fear is often the first and strongest influence. When money feels uncertain, fear enters as a protective response. It whispers warnings about running out, falling behind, or losing control. In this state, the mind becomes alert to threats rather than to opportunities. Decisions are filtered through a single question: *"How do I avoid pain right now?"* Instead of asking what is wise or sustainable, the fearful mind looks for immediate safety.

Under fear, people tend to rush decisions or avoid them entirely. Some spend quickly because holding money feels unsafe—it feels temporary, as though it will disappear anyway. Others freeze, afraid to make any choice at all, because choosing feels risky. In both cases, fear narrows perspective. It blocks long-term thinking and replaces it with short-term survival. What looks like poor judgment is often a nervous system trying to feel safe.

Pressure works differently but is just as powerful. Pressure comes from deadlines, expectations, responsibilities, and comparisons. Bills are due. The family needs support. Society sets timelines for success. Social media showcases progress that feels unreachable. Under pressure, money decisions stop being thoughtful and become reactive. The question shifts from *"What is right for me?"* to *"What do I need to do to relieve this tension?"*

Pressure creates urgency, and urgency weakens discernment. When a person feels pressured, they are more likely to accept unfavorable terms, take on unsustainable commitments, or chase quick solutions that promise relief. Long-term consequences are pushed aside in favor of short-term comfort. This is not because the person lacks wisdom, but because pressure compresses time and clouds judgment.

Confusion often follows fear and pressure. When financial information feels overwhelming or contradictory, confusion sets in. Advice comes from everywhere—friends, family, the internet—often pointing in different directions. Without a clear framework, the mind becomes overloaded. Too many options create paralysis. Too much information creates doubt.

In confusion, people often delay decisions, hoping clarity will appear on its own. Others make impulsive choices to escape the discomfort of not knowing what to do. Confusion makes simple actions feel complicated and complex actions feel impossible. It erodes confidence, leaving the person unsure of their ability to make good decisions.

These three forces—fear, pressure, and confusion—often reinforce one another. Fear heightens pressure. Pressure increases confusion. Confusion feeds fear. Together, they create a cycle where financial decisions are made from emotional strain rather than clarity. In this cycle, even good income or sound advice cannot produce lasting stability because the internal environment is not conducive to wise decision-making.

One of the most important insights this concept offers is that distorted financial decisions are not signs of irresponsibility. They are signs of overload. When the mind is under threat, rushed, or overwhelmed, it cannot access its full reasoning capacity. This is a human response, not a personal flaw.

Understanding this enables a powerful shift. Instead of trying to force better decisions through discipline alone, a person can begin by reducing fear, easing pressure, and simplifying confusion. Calm restores perspective. Space restores choice. Clarity restores confidence.

When fear is acknowledged rather than suppressed, it loses intensity. When pressure is examined rather than blindly obeyed, it becomes manageable. When confusion is met with patience rather than panic, understanding slowly emerges. In this calmer state, financial decisions become more intentional. The mind can weigh options. The body can relax. The future can be considered.

This is why true financial growth does not begin with stricter rules, but with a steadier inner environment. Decisions made from calm may not always be perfect, but they are rarely destructive. Over time, they build trust—trust in one's ability to think clearly, choose wisely, and respond thoughtfully.

Fear, pressure, and confusion distort financial decisions by hijacking the decision-making process. Clarity restores it. And clarity, once established, becomes the foundation upon which all sustainable economic progress is built.

Releasing Shame and Self-Blame Around Money

Shame is one of the quietest and most destructive forces in a person's financial life. Unlike fear, which feels loud and urgent, shame is subtle. It settles into the background of the mind and changes how a person sees themselves. Over time, financial struggle stops being something a person *experiences* and becomes something they *are*. Instead of thinking, *"I'm having money challenges,"* they begin to think, *"I'm bad with money."*

Self-blame grows from this place.

When money does not behave as expected—when it runs out, when bills pile up, when goals feel unreachable—the mind looks for an explanation. In the absence of understanding, it often turns inward. The person concludes that their struggle must mean they are irresponsible, careless, or incapable. These conclusions feel logical in a culture that praises financial success and quietly criticizes those who struggle, but they are rarely true.

Shame thrives when context is missing. Most people were never taught how to manage money in a structured, emotionally healthy way. They learned through observation, pressure, trial, and error. Yet when outcomes fall short, they judge themselves as though they were fully informed and fully equipped from the beginning. This mismatch between expectations and reality leads to unnecessary self-condemnation.

Self-blame also arises because money is deeply personal. It touches survival, dignity, responsibility, and independence. When someone struggles financially, it can feel like a reflection of their worth or adulthood. Over time, this internal judgment becomes habitual. The person may replay past mistakes repeatedly, reminding themselves of what they "should have done," without recognizing that those decisions were made with limited information and under emotional strain.

The problem with shame is not just how it feels—it is what it does. Shame shuts down curiosity. It discourages learning. It causes avoidance. A person who feels ashamed of their finances often avoids looking at numbers, avoiding conversations, and avoiding making plans. Not because they do not care, but because engaging with money feels emotionally painful. In this way, shame keeps financial problems alive by preventing honest engagement.

Releasing shame does not mean denying responsibility or pretending mistakes did not happen. It means placing responsibility in the right context. Responsibility becomes empowering when it is paired with understanding. Without understanding, responsibility becomes punishment.

When a person begins to see their financial history clearly, something important shifts. They recognize that many of their decisions were made under pressure, in fear, in confusion, or without guidance. They see that they were responding to circumstances, not failing at character. This does not erase consequences, but it softens the inner narrative. And when the inner narrative softens, change becomes possible.

Releasing self-blame also involves separating identity from behavior. A person can acknowledge, *"I made choices that did not help me,"* without concluding, *"I am the problem."* This distinction is crucial. Behavior can change. Identity, when attacked, resists. When people feel attacked internally, they either shut down or defend themselves. Neither leads to growth.

As shame loosens, a sense of emotional safety begins to return. Emotional safety allows honesty. Honesty allows awareness. Awareness allows choice. From this place, money stops feeling like a judgment and starts feeling like information. Numbers become data, not verdicts. Past mistakes become lessons, not life sentences.

This process takes time. Shame often developed over years of repetition—missed expectations, comparisons, and unspoken disappointment. Releasing it is not a single decision but a gradual reorientation. Each time a person chooses understanding over condemnation, they weaken shame's hold.

Ultimately, releasing shame and self-blame around money restores dignity. It reminds the reader that their bank balance never determines their worth. It creates the emotional space needed to learn, to plan, and to grow without fear of self-punishment. From this grounded place, financial responsibility becomes something a person can step into willingly, rather than something they feel forced to carry.

When shame leaves, clarity enters. When self-blame softens, confidence grows. And as confidence grows, money decisions begin to change—not because pressure has increased, but because understanding finally takes its place.

This is why releasing shame is not a side issue in financial growth. It is foundational.

CHAPTER 2

Scarcity Thinking and How It Shapes Your Life

Scarcity thinking is not simply the belief that there is not enough money. It is a way of seeing the world through the lens of limitation, uncertainty, and fear of loss. It is subtle, often invisible, and deeply influential. Many people live their entire lives under its influence without ever realizing it has a name—or that it can be changed.

At its core, scarcity thinking develops when a person's experience teaches them that resources are unstable. This may come from growing up in an environment where money was always tight, where bills caused tension, or where needs were met inconsistently. It may also come from sudden financial loss, prolonged uncertainty, or repeated disappointment. Over time, the mind learns to expect lack, even during moments of abundance.

Scarcity thinking does not always announce itself as fear. Often, it shows up as urgency. A constant sense that time is running out. Those opportunities must be grabbed immediately. That money must be used quickly before it disappears. In this mindset, patience feels dangerous, saving feels restrictive, and planning feels pointless. The future feels unreliable, so the present becomes everything.

This way of thinking quietly reshapes daily decisions. A person may spend money not because they are careless, but because holding onto it feels unsafe. They may struggle to invest in themselves because they fear wasting resources. They may reject opportunities that require time to mature, choosing immediate but smaller rewards instead. None of these choices feels irrational in the moment—they think necessary.

Scarcity thinking also affects how people value themselves. When resources feel limited, self-worth often becomes conditional. People begin to measure their value by productivity, usefulness, or survival. Rest feels undeserved. Enjoyment feels irresponsible. There is always a sense of needing to prove worth before receiving ease. This internal pressure creates exhaustion, even when progress is being made.

One of the most powerful effects of scarcity thinking is its tendency to narrow perception. When the mind is focused on what is missing, it loses sight of what is possible. Creativity diminishes. Risk feels threatening rather than strategic. Long-term planning feels unrealistic. The world begins to look smaller, more rigid, and more competitive. This narrowing does not stem from a lack of intelligence—it stems from prolonged exposure to uncertainty.

Scarcity thinking also shapes relationships. It can create comparison, jealousy, or resentment toward those who appear to have more. It can make collaboration feel risky, as though helping someone else reduces one's own chances. It can even affect generosity, not because the heart is closed, but because the mind believes there will not be enough left.

Importantly, scarcity thinking is not corrected by simply earning more money. Many people carry scarcity into higher income levels. They earn more, yet still feel anxious. They save more, yet still fear loss. This is because scarcity is not stored in the wallet; it is stored in expectations. Until expectation changes, behavior remains the same.

This chapter helps the reader understand that scarcity thinking is not a flaw. It is a learned response. The mind learned to protect itself in an unstable environment. That response may have been necessary at one time. But what protected the reader in the past may now be limiting their future.

Awareness is the turning point. When a person begins to notice scarcity thinking—how it influences decisions, emotions, and habits—they regain choice. They can pause before reacting. They can question urgency. They can separate real risk from imagined loss. Slowly, the grip of scarcity begins to loosen.

This chapter also introduces an important shift: moving from scarcity to sufficiency. Sufficiency does not mean excess or luxury. It means learning to recognize when there is *enough*—enough clarity, enough capacity, enough time to choose wisely. Sufficiency creates breathing room. It allows patience to return. It will enable planning to feel possible again.

As scarcity thinking fades, a person's life begins to expand—not necessarily in income at first, but in perspective. Decisions become calmer. The future feels less threatening. Money stops feeling like something to chase or fear and begins to feel like something to manage thoughtfully.

By the end of this chapter, the reader understands that scarcity thinking has shaped far more than their finances. It has shaped how they rest, how they choose, how they relate, and how they see themselves. And most importantly, they begin to see that scarcity is not who they are—it is something they learned.

And what is learned can be unlearned.

This realization becomes the bridge to the next stage of the journey: understanding how beliefs form, how they can be rewritten, and how a new relationship with money—and life—can be built on steadier ground.

The Psychology Behind Financial Limitation

Financial limitations are often misunderstood as surface-level problems—too little income, too many expenses, or poor opportunities. But beneath these visible factors lies a quieter force that shapes financial reality far more consistently: the human mind. Long before money problems appear on bank statements, they take root in perceptions, beliefs, emotional regulation, and learned patterns of behavior.

At a psychological level, the mind is designed to prioritize safety over growth. When a person experiences repeated financial uncertainty—whether due to poverty, instability, debt, or unpredictable income—the brain adapts, becoming alert, cautious, and protective. This adaptation is not a flaw; it is a survival response. However, what helps someone survive financial stress in the short term can limit them in the long term.

One of the most influential psychological mechanisms behind financial limitation is expectation. The mind forms expectations based on past experiences. If money has historically been scarce or unstable, the mind learns to expect loss. This expectation quietly shapes behavior. A person may hesitate to plan for the long term because the future feels unreliable. They may struggle to save because they expect money to disappear anyway. Even when income increases, the internal expectation of loss remains, guiding decisions beneath conscious awareness.

Another key factor is cognitive load. Financial stress consumes mental energy. When the mind is constantly calculating, worrying, or anticipating problems, it becomes overloaded. This overload reduces the brain's capacity for thoughtful decision-making. In such a state, people are more likely to rely on habits, impulses, or emotional shortcuts rather than deliberate planning. Over time, this reinforces patterns that keep finances constrained, even when better options exist.

Emotional regulation also plays a critical role. Money is deeply tied to emotion—fear, relief, pride, shame, and hope. When emotions are intense or unmanaged, they override rational thought. A person may spend to soothe anxiety, avoid finances to escape shame, or make rushed decisions under pressure. These behaviors are often labeled as irresponsibility, but psychologically, they are attempts to regulate emotional discomfort. Without healthier emotional tools, the same patterns repeat regardless of income level.

The psychology of identity further contributes to financial limitation. Many people unconsciously adopt identities such as "I'm not good with money" or "Money doesn't work for people like me." These identities influence how opportunities are perceived and acted upon. When someone believes financial competence is not part of who they are, they approach financial decisions with hesitation, self-doubt, or avoidance. Over time, these attitudes shape outcomes, reinforcing the original belief.

There is also the influence of learned helplessness—a psychological state that develops when repeated effort does not lead to improvement. If someone has tried to improve their finances multiple times without success, they may begin to believe that effort is pointless. This belief reduces motivation and initiative, not because the person lacks ambition, but because the mind has learned to conserve energy in the face of perceived futility.

Social comparison adds another psychological layer. Constant exposure to others' success—often without context—creates a distorted sense of normalcy. The mind begins to measure progress against unrealistic standards, leading to discouragement and impatience. From this emotional position, people may abandon steady growth in favor of risky shortcuts, or disengage altogether, both of which sustain financial limitation.

Importantly, psychological limitations are not permanent. It is adaptive, learned, and responsive to awareness. When a person begins to understand how past experiences have shaped their mind, they regain choice. They can pause, question assumptions, and respond rather than react. This awareness weakens the automatic patterns that once controlled decisions.

The psychology behind financial limitation teaches an essential truth: money does not fail people—unexamined mental patterns do. When the mind remains in survival mode, growth feels unsafe. When identity is tied to limitation, opportunity feels foreign. When emotions drive decisions, stability becomes fragile.

This understanding reframes the financial journey. It shifts the goal from simply earning more to becoming mentally and emotionally equipped to handle money wisely. It creates space for patience, learning, and intentional change. And it prepares the reader for the next stage of growth—rewriting beliefs, building discipline, and creating systems that support both financial and psychological stability.

In essence, financial limitation is not just about what is missing in the wallet. It is about what has been shaped in the mind. And when the mind changes, the financial story changes with it.

What Scarcity Mindset Really Means (Beyond Clichés)

The scarcity mindset is often reduced to a simple phrase: "*thinking there is not enough.*" While that definition is technically correct, it barely scratches the surface. In real life, scarcity mindset is not just a thought—it is a state of being, a way the mind and body organize themselves around perceived instability.

At its core, a scarcity mindset develops when a person learns, through experience, that resources are unreliable. It is not something people choose consciously. It is something they adapt into.

When money, time, love, opportunity, or safety have felt inconsistent or threatened, the mind learns to stay alert. It learns to watch closely. It learns to anticipate loss before it happens. Over time, this vigilance becomes normal. The person may no longer even feel afraid—scarcity becomes their baseline.

This is why the scarcity mindset is not always loud. It does not always sound like panic. Often, it sounds like urgency, overthinking, hesitation, or exhaustion.

A person with a scarcity mindset may work hard and still feel behind. They may save money and still feel unsafe. They may succeed outwardly while still feeling anxious internally. This is because the scarcity mindset is not about the amount of resources present—it is about trust in continuity. The underlying question is not *"Do I have enough right now?"* but *"Will this last?"*

A scarcity mindset trains the mind to focus on immediacy. The present moment feels fragile, so decisions are made to secure relief now, even if it comes at the cost of stability later. This is why people with a scarcity mindset may struggle with delayed gratification—not because they lack discipline, but because waiting feels dangerous. The future does not feel guaranteed, so the present becomes the only place that feels real.

Another misunderstood aspect of the scarcity mindset is that it often disguises itself as responsibility. A person may appear cautious, frugal, or overly careful, but beneath that behavior is fear of loss rather than clarity. They may avoid opportunities not because they are lazy or uninterested, but because risk feels unbearable. When resources have been scarce, the cost of failure feels too high.

The scarcity mindset also shapes how people interpret abundance. Instead of feeling calm or grateful, abundance can feel suspicious. When something good happens—extra money, a new opportunity, a season of ease—the mind may remain tense, waiting for the other shoe to drop. This is why some people feel more anxious during success than during struggle. Struggle is familiar. Stability is not.

Beyond money, a scarcity mindset affects time, energy, and self-worth. A person may feel they never have enough time, even when their schedule is full. They may feel they must constantly prove their value because worth feels conditional. Rest may feel undeserved. Saying no may feel risky. There is always a subtle pressure to keep going, keep holding on, keep surviving.

Importantly, a scarcity mindset is not a sign of weakness. It is a sign of adaptation. The mind adapted to environments where loss was possible or frequent. It learned to stay alert to protect the person. What once served as protection, however, can later become a limitation.

This is why simply telling someone to "think abundantly" rarely works. A scarcity mindset is not a surface-level belief that can be replaced with affirmations. It is embedded in emotional memory, nervous system responses, and lived experience. It loosens not through denial, but through safety, consistency, and understanding.

True healing from a scarcity mindset begins when a person recognizes it without judgment. When they can say, *"This way of thinking protected me once, but it no longer serves me,"* they regain choice. From there, the work is not to force abundance, but to rebuild trust—in systems, in self, and in the future.

This chapter helps the reader see that the scarcity mindset is not who they are. It is something they learned. And because it was understood, it can be gradually unlearned—not by pretending there is always enough, but by creating the conditions where enough begins to feel believable.

That is the real meaning of the scarcity mindset beyond clichés. It is not just about lack. It is about the expectation of loss.

And once that expectation changes, life begins to open again.

How Scarcity Forms Through Upbringing and Environment

Scarcity does not usually begin with a conscious belief. It starts with experience. Long before a person can name what money is or understand how it works, they are already learning how it *feels*. These early impressions, formed through upbringing and environment, quietly shape the way the mind relates to resources, safety, and stability for years to come.

In childhood, the world is interpreted emotionally rather than logically. A child may not understand income levels, economic conditions, or financial decisions, but they are highly sensitive to atmosphere. They notice tension when bills are discussed. They feel anxiety when resources are stretched. They sense relief when money arrives and fear when it leaves. Over time, these emotional cues teach the child whether the world feels predictable or uncertain.

When a child grows up in an environment where money is often scarce or unstable, the mind adapts. It learns that resources are fragile and that security cannot be taken for granted. This adaptation is not a flaw; it is a survival response. The child's nervous system becomes alert, scanning for signs of threat or loss. Later in life, this alertness may appear as anxiety, urgency, or difficulty relaxing around money—even when circumstances improve.

Scarcity can also form through repeated exposure to limiting messages. Phrases like "money doesn't last," "we can't afford that," or "people like us don't have money" are often spoken casually, without intention to harm. Yet when heard consistently, especially during formative years, they become internalized truths. The mind absorbs them as rules about reality, not opinions. These rules then shape expectations and behavior long after the original context has passed.

The environment plays an equally powerful role. Growing up in communities where opportunities are limited, where struggle is normalized, or where success feels distant can reinforce the belief that resources are scarce by nature. In such environments, planning for the future may feel unrealistic, and dreaming beyond immediate needs may feel unsafe. The focus becomes getting through the day, the week, or the month. This short-term orientation, while practical in the moment, can later limit long-term financial thinking.

Scarcity also arises from instability, not just from lack. Even households with a reasonable income can fall into scarcity thinking when money feels unpredictable. Sudden losses, inconsistent earnings, or financial crises teach the mind that stability can vanish without warning. In response, the mind learns to hold tightly, rush decisions, or avoid planning altogether. The lesson absorbed is not "we didn't have enough," but "what we have can disappear."

Social environment reinforces these lessons. Children observe how adults around them react to money—whether with calm, conflict, secrecy, or fear. They notice whether money is discussed openly or avoided entirely. Silence around money can be just as influential as stress. When questions are discouraged or finances are hidden, the child learns that money is something to fear or avoid, rather than understand.

As the child grows into adulthood, these early adaptations often remain active. The adult may feel uneasy about saving, spending, or investing in themselves without knowing why. They may feel pressure to use resources quickly or guilt when resources are used for rest or enjoyment. These reactions are echoes of earlier environments where security was uncertain.

Importantly, scarcity formed through upbringing is not a life sentence. It is learned, and what is learned can be unlearned. But unlearning does not begin with denial. It starts with recognition. When a person understands that circumstances beyond their control shaped their relationship with money, shame begins to soften. They can stop asking, *"What is wrong with me?"* and start asking, *"What did I learn, and does it still serve me?"*

This understanding brings compassion. It allows the reader to see their financial patterns not as personal failure, but as inherited responses that once made sense. From this place of compassion, change becomes possible—not through force, but through awareness and new experiences of stability.

Ultimately, scarcity, shaped by upbringing and environment, teaches the mind how to survive. But survival is not the same as growth. This chapter gently guides the reader toward that realization, preparing them to move from inherited limitation to intentional understanding. When the past is seen clearly, it no longer has to dictate the future.

That is how scarcity forms—and how it begins to loosen its grip.

Survival Mode vs Growth Mode Thinking

Survival mode and growth mode are not personality types. They are mental and emotional states shaped by experience, environment, and perceived safety. Most people move between these two modes at different points in life, often without realizing it. Understanding the difference between them is crucial because each mode produces very different decisions, habits, and financial outcomes.

Survival mode develops when life feels uncertain or threatening. This threat does not have to be dramatic. It can stem from prolonged financial stress, unstable income, mounting responsibilities, debt, or a constant sense of being behind. In survival mode, the mind's primary goal is simple: *get through today*. The future feels unreliable, so the present becomes the only focus.

When someone is thinking in survival mode, their attention narrows. The brain prioritizes immediate needs and short-term relief. Decisions are made quickly, often under pressure, because waiting feels risky. Saving money may feel pointless if the future feels uncertain. Planning long-term goals can feel unrealistic or even irresponsible when current needs are pressing. This is not because the person lacks vision, but because the mind is conserving energy in anticipation of perceived threats.

Emotionally, survival mode is accompanied by tension. There is often a sense of urgency in the background, even during calm moments. Rest feels undeserved. Pausing feels dangerous. There is a constant need to stay alert, productive, and prepared for the next problem. In this state, mistakes feel costly, and failure feels personal. The nervous system remains activated, making it difficult to think clearly or creatively.

Financially, survival mode leads to reactive behavior. Money decisions are driven by fear of loss or desire for immediate relief. A person may spend quickly because holding money feels unsafe, or avoid decisions entirely because choosing feels overwhelming. Even when opportunities arise, they may be dismissed because risk feels too high. Survival mode is focused on protection, not expansion.

Growth mode, by contrast, emerges when the mind feels safe enough to think beyond the present moment. Safety here does not mean wealth or comfort—it means predictability, clarity, and emotional stability. When a person feels that today is manageable, the mind can begin to ask different questions: *What can I build? What can I improve? What will matter later?*

In growth mode, thinking expands. The future becomes something that can be shaped rather than feared. Decisions are made with intention instead of urgency. Delayed gratification becomes possible because the future feels real and reachable. Planning feels empowering rather than overwhelming. There is room for patience, learning, and experimentation.

Emotionally, growth mode brings calm. There is less internal pressure to rush. Rest becomes restorative rather than guilt-inducing. Mistakes are seen as feedback instead of failure. Confidence grows—not because everything is perfect, but because the person trusts their ability to respond and adjust.

Financially, growth mode supports sustainable behavior. Money is viewed as a tool rather than a threat. Saving feels purposeful. Investing in skills or systems feels reasonable. Choices are guided by long-term benefit rather than short-term relief. Importantly, growth mode allows consistency. Progress may be slow, but it is steady.

The critical insight here is that growth mode cannot be forced while survival mode is active. Many people blame themselves for not thinking long-term, not saving, or not building wealth—without realizing that their mind is operating under survival conditions. Asking a survival-mode mind to plan for growth is like asking a person in danger to relax. The request misunderstands their current state.

This is why addressing financial struggle requires more than strategies. It requires creating conditions that allow the mind to shift out of survival mode. These conditions include clarity, order, emotional safety, and manageable expectations. As these conditions improve, growth mode emerges naturally.

Importantly, survival mode is not wrong. It is adaptive. It helped the person endure difficult seasons. But when survival mode becomes permanent, it limits what is possible. Growth requires a different internal environment—one where the mind is not constantly bracing for loss.

Understanding the difference between survival and growth thinking helps readers let go of self-judgment. It explains why certain habits felt necessary at one time and limiting at another. It also shows that shifting into growth mode is not about willpower, but about gradually creating stability and trust.

This concept prepares the reader for the rest of the journey. It explains why foundational work is necessary before introducing income strategies. Growth cannot be built on constant threat. It must be built on steadiness.

Survival mode helps you endure. Growth mode enables you to build.

Knowing when you are in each—and how to move from one to the other gently—is one of the most important skills a person can develop, not just financially, but in life.

How Scarcity Affects Spending, Saving, and Earning

Scarcity not only influences how much money a person has; it shapes how cash is handled at every stage—spent, saved, and earned. These behaviors are often judged in isolation, but in reality, they are expressions of the same internal environment. When scarcity is present, it touches all three.

Scarcity begins with the expectation that money is temporary, unreliable, or insufficient. Once that expectation settles in, it quietly directs behavior in ways that feel logical in the moment but are limiting over time.

When it comes to spending, scarcity often creates urgency. Money feels as though it must be used quickly before it disappears. This can show up as impulsive spending, emotional purchases, or difficulty delaying gratification. The expenditure is not always reckless—it is often driven by the belief that holding onto money does not guarantee safety. In a scarcity-driven mind, cash in hand feels unstable, so converting it into something tangible or immediately satisfying feels safer.

Scarcity can also lead to defensive spending. A person may spend on items that create a sense of control, comfort, or relief, especially after periods of stress. These purchases temporarily soothe anxiety or restore a sense of agency. Over time, however, they can create cycles of regret, reinforcing the belief that money is difficult to manage.

In other cases, scarcity leads to extreme restriction rather than spending. A person may avoid spending even on necessities, driven by fear of future lack. This can create constant tension and guilt around money, making every purchase feel risky. Whether spending too quickly or too cautiously, the underlying driver is the same: a lack of trust in continuity.

When it comes to saving, scarcity introduces contradiction. On one hand, the person may desperately want to save. On the other hand, saving can feel pointless or painful. If the future feels uncertain, saving for it feels like sacrificing the present for something that may never arrive. This internal conflict makes saving inconsistent or emotionally charged.

Scarcity also makes saved money feel unsafe. Instead of feeling reassuring, savings may trigger anxiety. A person may constantly worry about losing it, needing it suddenly, or being forced to spend it. In some cases, money saved with effort is eventually spent impulsively during moments of stress, not because it was unnecessary, but because the pressure becomes overwhelming.

This is why many people say they "can't keep savings." The issue is rarely discipline alone. It is the emotional relationship to saved money. Until saving feels like protection rather than deprivation, it doesn't remain easy to sustain.

Scarcity also has a profound effect on earnings. In a scarcity mindset, earning is often approached from fear rather than confidence. A person may underprice their skills out of fear of losing opportunities. They may avoid asking for better compensation because rejection feels too costly. They may cling to unstable income sources because familiar struggle feels safer than unfamiliar growth.

Scarcity can also limit earnings through short-term thinking. When the focus is on immediate survival, there is little energy left to invest in skill development, long-term growth, or strategic career decisions. Opportunities that require patience or delayed reward may be dismissed because they do not solve today's problem. Over time, this keeps earning potential constrained, even when the capability exists.

Another subtle effect of scarcity on earnings is exhaustion. Constant financial pressure drains mental and emotional energy. When a person is always trying to "make it through," creativity declines, confidence weakens, and initiative fades. This makes earning feel heavier than it needs to be, reinforcing the belief that money is hard to come by.

Across spending, saving, and earning, scarcity produces the same outcome: reactive rather than intentional behavior. Decisions are made to relieve discomfort rather than build stability. This is not a character flaw—it is a response to perceived instability.

Understanding this connection is powerful because it shifts the solution. Instead of trying to fix spending, saving, or earning separately, the reader begins to see that addressing scarcity at the root allows all three to change naturally. As trust in continuity grows, spending becomes more stable. When the future feels believable, saving becomes meaningful. When confidence replaces fear, earning expands.

This is why financial growth does not begin with stricter rules. Still, with a steadier internal environment, Scarcity affects money behaviors not because people are incapable, but because their minds are protecting them in the only way they know how.

When that protection is no longer needed, new patterns can emerge.

And when scarcity loosens its grip, spending, saving, and earning begin to align—not perfectly, but sustainably.

CHAPTER 3

Your Relationship With Money

Money is often treated as something external—numbers on a screen, notes in a wallet, figures to be earned, spent, or saved. Yet in reality, money is not just a resource people interact with; it is something they relate to. And, as with every relationship, the one a person has with money is shaped by experience, emotion, memory, and meaning. This chapter begins with a simple but powerful idea: everyone has a relationship with money, whether they are aware of it or not. That relationship influences decisions far more than logic alone ever could. It determines whether money feels calm or stressful, empowering or overwhelming, trustworthy or unstable.

For many people, money carries emotional meaning long before it carries practical function. It may represent safety—the reassurance that needs will be met. For others, it means fear—the constant worry of running out. Some experience money as control, something that determines choices and limits freedom. Others see it as validation, proof of success, adulthood, or worth. These meanings are rarely chosen consciously; they are inherited through lived experience.

When money is associated with safety, its absence triggers anxiety. Decisions are then made not to build wealth, but to reduce fear. When cash is associated with self-worth, financial difficulty feels like personal failure. When money is associated with control, losing it feels like losing stability in life itself. These emotional associations explain why money decisions often feel heavier than they should.

This chapter helps the reader understand that their reactions to money—avoidance, impulsiveness, over-caution, or obsession—are not random. They are responses shaped by how money has shown up in their life. A person who grew up watching money cause conflict may avoid financial conversations altogether. Someone who has experienced sudden loss may cling to money or struggle to trust it. Another who learned that money brought approval may chase it relentlessly, even at the cost of peace.

Over time, these emotional patterns form habits. Habits around spending, saving, and earning are not just behaviors—they are expressions of the relationship underneath. A person who overspends may be seeking comfort, relief, or a sense of control. A person who avoids budgeting may be protecting themselves from shame or anxiety. A person who undercharges for their work may be responding to fear of rejection or unworthiness.

One of the most important insights in this chapter is that money often becomes a stand-in for unmet emotional needs. It is used to soothe stress, feel secure, prove value, or escape discomfort. When money is asked to fulfill emotional roles it was never designed to carry, the relationship becomes strained. Money feels heavy. Decisions feel loaded. Peace feels conditional.

This chapter also explores how identity influences the relationship with money. Many people carry internal labels such as "I'm bad with money," "I'm not a financial person," or "Money never stays with me." These identities quietly shape behavior. When someone believes they are not capable with money, they approach financial decisions with hesitation or avoidance. Over time, this reinforces the original belief, creating a self-sustaining cycle.

Importantly, this chapter does not ask the reader to judge their relationship with money. It asks them to observe it. Observation brings awareness without shame. When a person can see how cash functions emotionally in their life, they gain distance from old patterns, money stops being something that happens *to* them, and becomes something they can relate to intentionally.

The chapter gently introduces the idea that a healthy relationship with money is neither fearful nor obsessive. It is respectful, balanced, and grounded. Money becomes a tool rather than a threat. It is neither avoided nor worshipped. It is managed with awareness and intention.

As the chapter unfolds, the reader begins to see that improving their financial life does not start with stricter rules or more pressure. It begins with understanding. Understanding how money has been experienced. Understanding what money has been asked to represent. Understanding where emotional weight has been placed on something that is meant to serve, not define.

By the end of this chapter, the reader is invited to shift their internal question. Instead of asking, *"How do I get more money?"* they begin to ask, *"How do I relate to money in a way that supports my life?"* That shift is subtle, but transformative.

This chapter prepares the ground for change. Once the relationship with money is understood, beliefs can be rewritten, habits can be reshaped, and systems can be built without resistance. Cash begins to feel lighter—not because circumstances have changed overnight, but because the internal struggle has softened.

A healthier relationship with money does not promise instant wealth. What it offers is something more foundational: clarity, calm, and the ability to make decisions without fear or self-judgment. And from that place, everything that follows becomes easier to build.

Money as Emotion, Identity, and Meaning

Money is often described as neutral—just numbers, currency, or a tool for exchange. But for most people, money has never been neutral. It carries emotion. It shapes identity. It holds meaning far beyond its practical use. Understanding this is essential because money problems are rarely just about money; they are about what money represents in a person's inner world.

From an emotional standpoint, money is often tied to safety. For many people, having money means breathing easier. It means protection from uncertainty, embarrassment, or dependency. When cash is present, the body relaxes. When it is absent, the body tightens. Anxiety rises, thoughts race, and decisions feel urgent. In this way, money becomes linked not just to comfort, but to survival itself.

When money is connected to emotional safety, its loss or instability triggers fear. That fear does not stay abstract—it shows up in behavior. A person may cling tightly to money, spend quickly to feel temporary relief, or avoid financial decisions altogether. These reactions are not irrational; they are emotional responses to perceived threat. The problem arises when money is expected to provide emotional security on its own, without the support of understanding, structure, or stability.

Money also becomes a container for emotions that have little to do with finances. Stress, exhaustion, loneliness, and pressure often manifest in money-related behavior. Spending may become a way to soothe discomfort. Earning may become a way to feel valuable. Saving may become a way to feel in control. In these moments, money is not being used as a tool—it is being used as an emotional regulator.

Beyond emotion, money plays a powerful role in identity. Many people unconsciously use money to answer the question, *"Who am I?"* Financial success may be interpreted as competence, adulthood, or worthiness. Financial struggle may be construed as failure, immaturity, or inadequacy. Over time, these interpretations become part of how a person sees themselves.

When money is tied to identity, financial ups and downs feel personal. A good month feels like validation. A bad month feels like rejection. The person is no longer just managing finances—they are managing their sense of self. This makes financial decisions more weighty and emotionally charged. Risk feels threatening not only because of potential loss, but because it threatens identity itself.

Identity-based money patterns often sound like quiet inner statements: *"I'm not good with money." "People like me don't get ahead." "I'll never be financially stable."* These statements are rarely questioned. They feel factual because they are familiar. Yet they shape behavior profoundly. When someone believes money competence is not part of who they are, they approach financial decisions with doubt, hesitation, or avoidance. Over time, behavior aligns with belief, reinforcing the identity.

Money also carries meaning shaped by culture, family, and personal history. For some, money means freedom—the ability to choose, rest, or explore. For others, it means responsibility—the weight of providing, supporting, or sacrificing. For some, it means power or control. For others, it means conflict, guilt, or loss. These meanings are formed through experience, not intention.

The meaning assigned to money determines how it is treated. If money means freedom, it may be pursued at the expense of balance. If it means responsibility, it may feel heavy and restrictive. If it implies conflict, it may be avoided altogether. In each case, money is responding to meaning, not logic.

The challenge arises when money is asked to fulfill roles it was never designed to carry. Money cannot provide self-worth. It cannot resolve emotional wounds. It cannot create lasting safety on its own. When these expectations are placed on money, the relationship becomes strained. Cash begins to feel demanding, unpredictable, or never enough—not because it is insufficient, but because it is being asked to do too much.

This chapter concept helps the reader gently separate money from these deeper roles. It invites them to see that while money interacts with emotion, identity, and meaning, it need not define them. Emotional safety can be built through clarity and structure. Identity can be grounded in values and capability rather than income. Meaning can be drawn from purpose and alignment rather than numbers.

When this separation begins, money becomes lighter. Decisions feel less personal. Mistakes become learning moments rather than verdicts. Success becomes something to steward rather than cling to. Cash returns to its proper place—as a tool that supports life, not a force that determines worth.

Understanding money as emotion, identity, and meaning is not about rejecting these connections; it is about recognizing them. It is about becoming aware of them. Awareness restores choice. And with choice, a person can begin to build a healthier, more balanced relationship with money—one where money serves life rather than silently shaping it.

This understanding prepares the reader for the deeper work ahead: rewriting beliefs, reshaping habits, and building systems that honor both emotional reality and practical wisdom.

Money as Safety, Fear, Control, or Self-Worth

Money rarely exists as a simple tool in human life. For most people, it quietly takes on emotional roles shaped by experience, environment, and unmet needs. Over time, money begins to stand in for things it was never meant to provide. It becomes safety. It becomes fear. It becomes control. It becomes self-worth. Understanding these roles is essential because they influence financial behavior far more than knowledge or intention ever could.

For many people, money represents safety. Safety means stability, predictability, and protection from uncertainty. When someone has experienced financial instability—missed bills, sudden loss, dependency, or insecurity—the mind learns to associate money with survival. In this state, having money brings relief, while lacking it triggers anxiety. The nervous system responds as though something essential is at risk.

When money is tied to safety, decisions are often driven by fear of losing that sense of protection. A person may hoard money, struggle to spend even on necessities, or feel constant anxiety regardless of how much they have. Saving may not feel reassuring; it may feel fragile. The underlying issue is not money itself, but the belief that safety exists only as long as money does. This places enormous emotional weight on finances, making peace feel conditional.

Money can also function as fear. Instead of representing protection, it becomes a source of threat. For those who grew up around financial conflict, instability, or shame, money may feel dangerous. It may represent arguments, pressure, or constant worry. In this role, money is something to avoid rather than understand.

When money is associated with fear, people may delay financial decisions, avoid looking at numbers, or disengage from planning altogether. Ignoring money feels safer than confronting the emotions it triggers. This avoidance is often misinterpreted as irresponsibility, but at its core, it is emotional self-protection. The mind is trying to avoid discomfort, not sabotage success.

Money can also serve as a form of control. In environments where life felt unpredictable, money may have become one of the few things that offered a sense of agency—having money meant having choices. Losing money meant losing power. In this dynamic, money becomes tightly linked to control over life itself.

When money is used as control, financial decisions can become rigid or extreme. A person may micromanage every expense, struggle to trust others with shared finances, or feel intense anxiety when money is spent outside their plan. On the other hand, they may use money to control outcomes—overworking to maintain control or spending to assert independence. In both cases, money is used to manage uncertainty rather than to live calmly.

Perhaps the most emotionally charged role money plays is self-worth. Many people unconsciously measure their value by their financial status. Success feels like validation. Struggle feels like failure. Over time, money becomes a mirror reflecting how a person thinks about themselves. This is especially common in cultures that equate achievement with income and independence.

When money is tied to self-worth, financial ups and downs become deeply personal. A raise feels like approval. A setback feels like rejection. The person is no longer just managing resources; they are managing their sense of identity. This makes financial decisions emotionally heavy and increases the fear of mistakes. Risk feels dangerous not only because of potential loss, but because it threatens the person's sense of value.

These roles—safety, fear, control, and self-worth—are not chosen deliberately. They develop gradually as the mind tries to make sense of the world. At one time, they may have served a purpose. They may have helped a person survive uncertainty, cope with stress, or feel some sense of stability. But when money is asked to carry these roles indefinitely, it becomes overloaded.

Money cannot provide emotional safety on its own. Money cannot resolve fear at its root. Money cannot create lasting control over life. Money cannot define human worth.

When it is forced into these roles, it begins to feel heavy, unstable, or never enough. Decisions become reactive. Peace becomes conditional. The relationship with money grows tense.

This concept invites the reader to separate money from these emotional responsibilities gently. Safety can be built through understanding and structure. Fear can be addressed through clarity and support. Control can be replaced with trust and systems. Self-worth can be grounded in values, capability, and growth rather than numbers.

As this separation begins, money returns to its proper place. It becomes a tool rather than a threat. A resource rather than a measure of worth. Something to manage thoughtfully rather than cling to or avoid.

Understanding money in this way does not remove responsibility—it restores balance. It allows the reader to engage with money calmly, make decisions without emotional overload, and build financial stability on a foundation that does not collapse under pressure.

This shift is not instant, but it is transformative. When money stops carrying emotional weight it was never meant to hold, it becomes far easier to work with—and far less powerful over one's life.

Emotional Spending and Avoidance

Emotional spending and financial avoidance are two of the most misunderstood behaviors around money. They are often labeled as irresponsibility, lacking discipline, or having poor self-control. In reality, they are rarely about money at all. They are about emotion, regulation, and protection.

At their core, both behaviors arise from the same place: discomfort. The discomfort may come from stress, fear, shame, exhaustion, or a sense of being overwhelmed. Money becomes the stage on which these emotions play out, not because money causes them, but because money is closely tied to survival, identity, and control.

Emotional spending occurs when money is used to manage feelings rather than meet practical needs. A person may spend to feel relief after a difficult day, to regain a sense of control when life feels chaotic, or to escape feelings of lack or inadequacy momentarily. The purchase itself is not the true goal. The emotional shift it provides—comfort, distraction, validation, or relief—is what the mind is seeking.

This is why emotional spending often happens even when the person knows it is not helpful. In the moment, logic is secondary. The nervous system is looking for soothing. The act of spending provides a brief sense of agency: *I chose this. I did something.* That feeling, even if temporary, can feel stabilizing when emotions are intense.

Afterward, however, emotional spending often brings guilt or regret. The short-term relief fades, and the original emotion returns—sometimes stronger than before. This creates a cycle: discomfort leads to spending, spending leads to shame, and shame increases discomfort. Over time, the person may begin to see themselves as "bad with money," reinforcing self-blame without addressing the true cause.

On the other end of the spectrum lies financial avoidance. Instead of engaging with money to manage emotion, the person disengages entirely. Bills go unopened. Bank balances go unchecked. Budgets are postponed. Financial conversations are avoided. This behavior is often mistaken for carelessness or denial, but its root is usually emotional pain.

Avoidance develops when money triggers anxiety, shame, or a sense of failure. Looking at numbers feels overwhelming. Making decisions feels risky. The mind chooses distance as a form of protection. If I don't look, I don't have to feel. In this way, avoidance becomes a coping mechanism.

Ironically, avoidance often increases the very stress it is trying to prevent. Unchecked problems grow. Deadlines pass. Consequences accumulate. Yet the mind continues to avoid because engaging still feels emotionally unsafe. This creates a sense of paralysis that can be deeply discouraging.

Both emotional spending and avoidance are responses to emotional overload. When the nervous system is under constant pressure—financial, relational, or psychological—it seeks ways to regulate itself. Some people regulate through action (spending). Others regulate through withdrawal (avoidance). Neither approach is inherently wrong. They are attempts to cope with discomfort using the tools available at the time.

What makes these patterns persistent is the lack of awareness. When a person believes their behavior is "bad," they focus on control rather than understanding. They try to force discipline without addressing the emotional trigger. This often fails, reinforcing the belief that they lack willpower.

Understanding emotional spending and avoidance reframes the problem. It shifts the question from *"Why can't I control myself?"* to *"What am I trying to soothe or avoid?"* This shift is powerful. It opens the door to compassion and curiosity instead of punishment.

When emotions are acknowledged rather than suppressed, they lose intensity. When money is approached with gentleness rather than judgment, engagement becomes possible. Small acts of awareness—pausing before a purchase, noticing tension when checking an account—begin to weaken old patterns.

This does not mean emotional spending or avoidance disappears overnight. These behaviors developed to meet real needs. Releasing them requires building alternative ways to feel safe, soothed, and supported. As emotional capacity grows, money no longer needs to carry the weight of regulation.

Ultimately, emotional spending and avoidance are not signs of financial failure. They are signs of unmet emotional needs and prolonged pressure. When those needs are addressed through understanding, structure, and patience, money behaviors naturally begin to change. Money becomes less reactive. Decisions become more intentional. And the relationship with money grows steadier—not because emotion is gone, but because it is no longer in control.

This understanding prepares the reader for the next step: learning to relate to money consciously rather than unconsciously, and to build habits that support both emotional well-being and financial stability.

Why People Sabotage Financial Progress

Financial self-sabotage is one of the most confusing experiences people face. A person may finally start saving, earning more, or gaining clarity—only to make choices that undo that progress. From the outside, it looks irrational. From the inside, it often feels automatic, even inevitable.

The key to understanding financial self-sabotage is this: people rarely sabotage what feels safe to keep. Progress is not always comforting. For many, it is unfamiliar, threatening, or emotionally destabilizing.

At a deeper level, the mind prioritizes *emotional safety* over financial improvement. If progress disrupts the internal balance a person has learned to survive with, the mind may resist—even if the change is objectively positive.

One of the most common reasons people sabotage progress is identity mismatch. If someone has lived for years seeing themselves as "struggling," "behind," or "bad with money," improvement creates tension. The new reality does not align with the old identity.

Subconsciously, the mind tries to restore familiarity. Spending the savings, avoiding the plan, or walking away from opportunity brings things back to what feels known—even if that known state is difficult.

Another powerful driver is fear of loss. For someone shaped by instability, progress feels fragile. When money increases, anxiety may increase with it. The thought is not always conscious, but it is persistent: *"What if I lose this?"* To avoid the pain of potential loss, the mind may choose to end progress early, on its own terms. Losing by choice feels safer than losing by surprise.

There is also the fear of greater responsibility. Financial growth brings new expectations—better decisions, consistency, planning, boundaries. For someone already overwhelmed, this can feel like too much. Sabotage then becomes an escape from pressure. Returning to struggle feels easier than sustaining growth that demands more structure and discipline.

Shame plays a quiet but central role as well. When someone carries unresolved shame about past financial mistakes, success can feel undeserved. Improvement triggers thoughts like, *"Who do I think I am?"* or *"I'll mess this up anyway."* Sabotage then becomes a way to confirm the shame-based belief and relieve the discomfort of feeling unworthy.

Another overlooked factor is emotional regulation. Many people have learned to manage stress through financial behaviors—spending for comfort, avoiding decisions to reduce anxiety, and staying busy to survive. When progress begins, those coping mechanisms are threatened. The mind resists losing them, even if they are unhealthy. Sabotage restores familiar emotional patterns.

There is also the influence of learned helplessness. After repeated attempts that did not lead to lasting improvement, some people lose trust in progress. Even when things improve, they expect collapse. This expectation quietly guides behavior. Planning feels pointless. Discipline feels temporary. Sabotage confirms what the mind already believes: *"This never lasts."*

Importantly, financial self-sabotage is not always dramatic. It can be subtle:

- Skipping tracking "just this once."
- Making one unplanned decision that breaks momentum
- Delaying a necessary conversation
- Ignoring a boundary that was working

These small breaks in consistency often feel harmless, but they reopen old patterns. Understanding self-sabotage changes the response. Instead of increasing punishment or pressure, the solution is to build internal safety. Progress must feel emotionally tolerable before it can be sustained.

This means:

- Expanding identity to include stability
- Normalizing consistency
- Reducing pressure around "doing it perfectly."
- Creating systems that support the nervous system, not fight it

When progress is paired with calm, patience, and self-trust, sabotage loses its purpose. The mind no longer needs to pull the emergency brake.

Ultimately, people sabotage financial progress not because they want to fail, but because part of them is still trying to stay safe. When safety is rebuilt internally, progress no longer feels threatening—it feels natural.

And when progress feels natural, it finally lasts.

Separating Money from Identity and Validation

One of the most damaging yet invisible dynamics in a person's financial life is the moment money becomes tied to identity and validation. At that point, money stops being a tool and starts becoming a mirror—reflecting how a person feels about themselves, their worth, their success, and their place in the world.

When money and identity are fused, financial outcomes are no longer just outcomes. They become personal judgments.

A good month feels like proof of competence. A bad month feels like proof of failure. Progress feels like validation. Struggle feels like rejection.

This emotional attachment makes money far heavier than it needs to be.

For many people, this connection forms gradually. In childhood or early adulthood, money often comes to be associated with responsibility, independence, and adulthood. Being able to earn, provide, or contribute may have been praised. Needing help, falling short, or struggling may have been criticized—sometimes openly, sometimes subtly. Over time, the mind absorbs the message that *being financially stable equals being worthy*, while struggling financially equals being inadequate.

Once this belief settles in, money becomes a scorecard for identity. People begin to ask questions like:

- "What does my income say about me?"
- "What does my financial struggle mean about my intelligence or discipline?"
- "If I were really capable, wouldn't I be further by now?"

These questions are rarely asked consciously, yet they constantly influence emotion and behavior.

When money is tied to validation, decisions become emotionally charged. Financial mistakes feel humiliating rather than instructive. Asking for help feels like weakness rather than wisdom. Learning feels threatening because it confirms that something is missing. Growth becomes stressful because it raises the stakes of failure.

In this state, money is no longer just money. It becomes a symbol of personal worth.

This is why some people avoid looking at their finances—not because they don't care, but because the numbers feel like a judgment. It is also why others chase money relentlessly—not because they love wealth, but because they are seeking reassurance that they are "enough."

Validation-driven money patterns often manifest as overworking, undercharging, people-pleasing, or endless comparisons with others. The person is not just trying to earn—they are trying to prove themselves. This makes financial progress exhausting and fragile. No amount of money ever feels like enough, because the underlying need is not economic—it is emotional.

Separating money from identity begins with a crucial realization: money reflects circumstances and skills, not human value. Income is influenced by opportunity, timing, education, environment, and access—not just effort or intelligence. Financial outcomes are feedback, not verdicts.

When a person understands this, something softens internally. Mistakes stop feeling like evidence of failure and start feeling like part of learning. Progress becomes something to steward rather than cling to. Setbacks become information rather than shame.

This separation also restores emotional safety. When worth is no longer tied to numbers, a person can engage with money more honestly. They can look at their finances without self-attack. They can make adjustments without feeling exposed. They can plan without pressure to prove anything.

Importantly, separating money from validation does not remove ambition or responsibility. It strengthens them. A person who no longer needs money to define their worth can make clearer decisions. They can choose growth paths that align with their values rather than their insecurities. They can pace themselves without fear of falling behind others.

This shift also reduces self-sabotage. When money is no longer a measure of identity, progress no longer threatens the self. Success feels safe to keep. Stability feels allowed. There is no internal need to return to struggle to preserve a familiar self-image.

At its core, this concept restores dignity. It reminds the reader that their worth existed before their income and will remain regardless of it. Money becomes something they manage—not something that manages them.

When money is separated from identity and validation, financial life becomes calmer, lighter, and more sustainable. Decisions are guided by clarity rather than emotion. Growth is motivated by purpose rather than fear. And money finally returns to its proper role—as a tool that supports life, not a mirror that defines it.

This separation is not a denial of reality. It is a reclaiming of perspective.

And once perspective is restored, financial freedom becomes far more than a number—it becomes a state of inner stability that money can finally support instead of distort.

CHAPTER 4

Rewriting Your Financial Belief System

Every person carries a financial belief system, whether they realize it or not. It is the collection of ideas, assumptions, and expectations they hold about money—how it behaves, what it does, and what it says about them. This belief system quietly guides financial decisions far more powerfully than logic, advice, or intention.

This chapter exists because belief always precedes behavior. Long before a person spends, saves, earns, or avoids money, they are acting on what they believe to be true. If those beliefs were formed in environments of scarcity, instability, or confusion, they will continue to produce the same outcomes—even when circumstances change.

Rewriting the financial belief system does not mean forcing positive thinking or denying reality. It means becoming aware of inherited beliefs, questioning whether they are still accurate, and replacing them with grounded, supportive truths that align with how money actually works.

Most financial beliefs are not consciously chosen. They are absorbed early and reinforced repeatedly. A person may believe, without ever stating it directly, that money is difficult to keep, that it disappears quickly, or that stability is temporary. Others may think they are "not financial people," or that money always comes with stress, conflict, or loss. These beliefs feel factual because they were learned through lived experience.

The problem is not that these beliefs once existed. The problem is that they remain unexamined.

This chapter helps the reader see that beliefs formed under pressure were designed for survival, not sustainability. A belief such as *"Money doesn't last"* may have helped a person stay alert in an unstable environment. But when carried into adulthood, it creates anxiety around saving, planning, and long-term growth. The belief continues to shape decisions even when it no longer serves its purpose.

Rewriting a belief begins with awareness. The chapter guides the reader to notice the automatic thoughts that appear around money—especially during stress. These thoughts often sound absolute: *always, never, people like me, it won't work*. When these statements become conscious, they lose some of their power. What was once assumed becomes something that can be examined.

The chapter then introduces an essential psychological shift: beliefs are interpretations, not truths. They feel true because they are familiar, not because they are accurate. This realization is liberating. It allows the reader to step back from their financial story and ask a new question: *"Is this belief describing reality, or describing my past?"*

Rewriting does not happen by replacing one extreme with another. Scarcity beliefs are not healed by exaggerated optimism. Instead, they are replaced with stable, reality-based principles. For example, instead of believing *"Money never stays,"* the new belief becomes *"Money stays where there is structure and awareness."* This belief is not wishful—it is practical and observable.

This chapter emphasizes that new beliefs must be livable. They must feel emotionally tolerable to the nervous system. A belief that feels unrealistic will be rejected internally, even if it sounds positive. Rewriting works when beliefs are adjusted gradually, in ways that the mind can accept as safe and plausible.

The chapter also addresses resistance. Many people unconsciously resist changing financial beliefs because those beliefs are tied to identity and safety. Letting go of old beliefs can feel like letting go of familiarity. This chapter normalizes that resistance and reframes it as protection rather than failure. Awareness creates patience, and patience creates room for change.

Another important aspect of rewriting beliefs is the consistency of reinforcement. A single insight does not change beliefs. They are changed through repeated experience. Each time the reader notices a financial decision made calmly, each time money is handled with awareness rather than fear, a new belief is strengthened. Over time, behavior and belief begin to align.

This chapter also helps the reader understand that belief rewriting is not about perfection. Old beliefs may resurface under stress. This does not mean failure—it means the system is still learning. The goal is not to eliminate all scarcity thoughts, but to reduce their authority. When a belief no longer automatically controls behavior, it has already lost its dominance.

By the end of this chapter, the reader begins to experience money differently—not because their circumstances have changed, but because their interpretation has. Money feels less threatening. Decisions feel more intentional. The internal dialogue around finances becomes calmer and more grounded.

This chapter marks a turning point in the book. Earlier chapters focused on understanding how struggle formed, how scarcity operates, and how money became emotional. This chapter begins the reconstruction phase. It prepares the reader to move from awareness into stability, from reaction into choice.

Rewriting the financial belief system does not promise instant wealth. What it promises is something far more foundational: a mind that no longer works against economic growth. And when the mind is aligned, learning how to earn, manage, and sustain money becomes not only possible but sustainable.

This is why this chapter matters. Without rewritten beliefs, new strategies collapse. With rewritten beliefs, progress finally has somewhere safe to land.

From Inherited Beliefs to Chosen Principles

Most people live their financial lives guided by beliefs they never consciously selected. These beliefs were inherited—absorbed from family, culture, environment, and experience—long before the person had the awareness or capacity to evaluate them. Over time, these inherited beliefs begin to feel like facts about reality rather than interpretations shaped by circumstance.

This chapter concept begins with a simple but powerful distinction: beliefs are what we absorb; principles are what we choose.

Inherited beliefs are formed passively. A child hears repeated statements about money. They observe how adults react to bills, income, loss, or opportunity. They notice whether money creates calm or conflict, security or anxiety. From these observations, the mind concludes—not consciously, but instinctively. These conclusions become internal rules about how money works and what is possible.

Because inherited beliefs are formed early and reinforced repeatedly, they feel deeply personal. They often operate without language. A person may never say, *"Money disappears,"* yet still behave as if it does. They may never say, *"I'm not meant to be financially stable,"* yet unconsciously make decisions that align with that assumption. Inherited beliefs guide behavior quietly, beneath awareness.

The limitation of inherited beliefs is not that they were wrong at the time. Many of them made sense in the environments where they formed. Believing that money is unstable may have helped a person stay alert during uncertain periods. Believing that resources must be used quickly may have been practical when future access was unpredictable. These beliefs were adaptive—they helped the person cope.

The problem arises when these beliefs persist long after the original conditions have changed.

This is where chosen principles come in.

Principles are not emotional reactions. They are grounded understandings about how life and money actually function. Unlike beliefs, principles are selected consciously. They are based on clarity rather than conditioning. A principle does not depend on mood, fear, or familiarity—it provides a steady guide even when emotions fluctuate.

Moving from inherited beliefs to chosen principles requires awareness. The person must first recognize that what they believe about money may be inherited rather than intentional. This recognition alone is powerful. It creates distance between the self and the belief. The belief is no longer *who I am*; it becomes *something I learned*.

Once this distance exists, choice becomes possible.

For example, an inherited belief might say, *"Money never lasts."* A chosen principle reframes this as, *"Money stays where there is structure, awareness, and discipline."* The principle does not deny experience—it explains it. It replaces emotional certainty with practical understanding.

Another inherited belief might say, *"I'm bad with money."* A chosen principle responds, *"Financial skill is learned, not innate."* This principle removes identity from the equation and restores agency. It allows growth without shame.

What makes principles powerful is their stability. Beliefs can shift with emotion. Principles remain consistent. A person may feel afraid and still act according to principle. They may feel uncertain and still choose discipline. Principles do not require emotional comfort to function—they provide direction even when emotions are unsettled.

This chapter emphasizes that choosing principles is not about rejecting the past. It is about honoring it while refusing to be controlled by it. Inherited beliefs can be acknowledged with compassion: *"This belief protected me once."* Chosen principles then take responsibility for the future: *"This principle will guide me now."*

Another important aspect of this transition is realism. Chosen principles must be believable. If a principle feels exaggerated or unrealistic, the mind will reject it. This is why principles are not affirmations. They are grounded truths that can be observed in real life. They feel steady, not forced.

Over time, principles reshape behavior. When decisions are made repeatedly from principle rather than belief, new experiences are created. These experiences gradually weaken old beliefs and strengthen new patterns. The change is not dramatic, but it is durable.

This shift also restores dignity. Instead of being driven by unconscious scripts, the reader becomes an active participant in their financial life. They are no longer reacting to inherited expectations—they are responding from chosen understanding.

By the end of this concept, the reader realizes something essential: they are not required to live by beliefs they did not choose. They can examine what they inherited, keep what serves them, and release what limits them. In its place, they can build a personal financial framework rooted in clarity, responsibility, and self-trust.

This movement—from inherited beliefs to chosen principles—is not just a financial shift. It is a maturation process. It marks the transition from survival to stewardship, from reaction to intention, and from unconscious repetition to conscious direction.

And once this transition begins, every financial decision that follows is made from a place of greater stability and freedom.

Common Money Beliefs That Keep People Stuck

Money beliefs are not random thoughts. They are internal rules about how money works, what is possible, and where a person fits within that reality. These rules often operate silently, shaping decisions and behavior without ever being questioned. When financial progress feels difficult despite effort, it is usually because one or more of these beliefs is still running in the background.

One of the most common limiting beliefs is the idea that "money never stays." This belief is usually formed through repeated experience rather than logic. When money has historically disappeared quickly due to bills, emergencies, or instability, the mind learns to expect loss. Even when income increases, the expectation remains. As a result, saving feels pointless, planning feels fragile, and spending often happens quickly—not out of recklessness, but because holding money feels unsafe. The belief creates a self-fulfilling loop in which money leaves because it is expected to.

Another deeply rooted belief is "I'm bad with money." This belief ties financial behavior directly to identity. Instead of seeing money skills as learnable, the person sees them as innate traits they lack. This belief discourages learning, experimentation, and patience. Mistakes feel like confirmation rather than part of growth. Over time, the person avoids engagement with money altogether, reinforcing the belief they started with.

Many people are also held back by the belief that "more money will fix everything." While this belief seems hopeful, it can be limiting. It postpones responsibility and awareness. Instead of learning how to manage, structure, and relate to money, the person waits for income to change their reality. When income increases, but habits and beliefs remain the same, disappointment follows. The belief keeps the person focused on external rescue rather than internal readiness.

Another common belief is "people like me don't get ahead." This belief is often shaped by environment, culture, or repeated comparison. It may be tied to background, education, geography, or past outcomes.

While it may feel realistic, it subtly restricts possibilities. Opportunities are dismissed before they are explored. Effort is reduced because success feels unlikely. The belief protects against disappointment but also prevents progress.

The belief "money is stressful and always comes with problems" is also widespread. For those who grew up around financial conflict, money may be associated with tension, arguments, or emotional strain. As adults, these individuals may unconsciously avoid financial growth because growth feels like inviting more stress. Stability feels suspicious. Money becomes something to manage minimally rather than build intentionally.

Another belief that keeps people stuck is "I must get it right or not try at all." This perfection-based belief creates paralysis. Financial decisions are delayed because the fear of making a mistake feels too costly. Planning feels overwhelming. Instead of learning through small, imperfect steps, the person waits for clarity that never fully arrives. Inaction then reinforces the belief that money is too complex or intimidating.

Some people carry the belief that "wanting money makes me greedy or selfish." This belief often comes from moral or cultural messages absorbed early in life. It creates internal conflict between desire and values. As a result, the person may unconsciously limit earnings, undercharge for their work, or feel guilty for wanting financial improvement. Progress becomes emotionally uncomfortable, and sabotage may follow.

Another subtle but powerful belief is "I should already be further by now." This belief is rooted in comparison and expectation rather than reality. It creates chronic dissatisfaction and impatience. Instead of building steadily, the person feels behind and rushed. Decisions are made to catch up rather than to build wisely. When results do not come quickly, discouragement sets in, reinforcing the belief of inadequacy.

What all these beliefs have in common is that they feel true because they are familiar, not because they are accurate. They were formed through experience, repetition, and emotional association. They once helped the person make sense of their environment. But when left unexamined, they continue to shape outcomes long after the original conditions have changed.

This concept is not about blaming beliefs for everything. It is about recognizing that beliefs create filters. They determine what a person notices, attempts, avoids, or dismisses. When beliefs are limiting, behavior follows suit—often without conscious intention.

The power of this chapter lies in awareness. When a belief is brought into the open, it loses some of its authority. The reader can ask, *"Is this belief describing reality, or describing my past?"* That question alone creates space for change.

Understanding common money beliefs that keep people stuck is not about replacing them with unrealistic optimism. It is about replacing them with grounded principles that reflect how money actually works: that skill is learned, stability is built, and progress comes from structure, not luck or identity.

Once these beliefs are clearly seen, they no longer automatically control behavior. And when belief loosens its grip, movement becomes possible.

This sets the stage for the next step in the journey: consciously choosing new financial principles that support growth instead of repeating the past.

How Beliefs Influence Decisions Unconsciously

Most financial decisions are not made consciously. They are created automatically, guided by beliefs that operate beneath awareness. This is why people often repeat the same patterns even after learning new information or setting new intentions. Knowledge alone does not drive behavior. Belief does.

At an unconscious level, beliefs act like filters. They determine what the mind notices, what it ignores, what feels safe, and what feels risky. Long before a person evaluates options logically, their belief system has already narrowed the field of acceptable choices.

For example, if someone unconsciously believes that money is unstable, their mind remains on the lookout for signs of loss. Opportunities that require patience may feel unsafe. Saving may feel pointless. Spending may feel urgent. None of this feels like a belief in action—it feels like common sense. That is the power of unconscious belief: it presents interpretation as reality.

Beliefs form early and are reinforced through repetition. When an experience occurs often enough—money running out, plans failing, effort not paying off—the mind stops questioning it. The pattern becomes expected. Once expected, it becomes automatic. The belief no longer needs to announce itself. It simply directs behavior quietly.

This is why people sometimes say, *"I don't know why I did that."* The decision was not random. It was guided by an internal rule that never entered conscious thought.

Unconscious beliefs also influence emotional responses, which, in turn, influence choice. Before a decision is made, the body reacts. Tension, anxiety, urgency, or avoidance arise instantly. These sensations are not created by the situation alone—they are created by what the mind believes the situation means. The person then decides to relieve or respond to that emotion, often without realizing that the belief triggered it.

This process happens quickly:

- A situation appears
- A belief interprets it
- An emotion is activated
- A decision is made

By the time logic enters, the decision often already feels justified. Another way beliefs influence decisions unconsciously is through identity alignment. The mind prefers consistency. It resists choices that contradict how a person sees themselves. If someone believes they are "bad with money," they will unconsciously avoid behaviors that would challenge that identity. Planning, tracking, or investing may feel uncomfortable—not because they are difficult, but because they conflict with the internal story.

Similarly, if someone believes financial stability is not meant for people like them, they may unconsciously reject opportunities, delay action, or disengage when progress begins. These behaviors protect identity familiarity, even when that identity is limiting.

Beliefs also shape risk perception. Two people can face the same opportunity and feel completely different levels of threat. One sees possibility; the other sees danger. The difference is not intelligence—it is belief. The belief determines whether uncertainty feels exciting or frightening. Decisions then follow the emotional signal, not the objective facts.

Importantly, unconscious beliefs are efficient. The brain uses them to conserve energy. Constantly evaluating every decision consciously would be exhausting. Beliefs allow the mind to operate on autopilot. The problem arises when outdated beliefs remain in control. They continue to guide decisions based on past conditions rather than present reality.

This is why willpower alone rarely creates lasting change. Willpower operates at the conscious level. Beliefs operate beneath it. When the two conflict, belief usually wins. The person may try to act differently, but the internal discomfort eventually pulls them back to familiar patterns.

Change begins when beliefs are brought into awareness. When a person notices their automatic reactions and asks, *"What must I believe for this decision to feel right?"* they interrupt the unconscious process. The belief is no longer invisible. Once seen, it can be examined.

Crucially, this does not mean all beliefs must be removed. It means outdated beliefs must be updated. Beliefs that once protected survival may now limit growth. Awareness allows the person to choose whether a belief still serves them.

As new beliefs are practiced consciously—through small, consistent decisions—the unconscious mind begins to adjust. The emotional response softens. Decisions feel less charged. What once required effort becomes natural. This is how belief change becomes embodied rather than forced.

Understanding how beliefs influence decisions unconsciously restores self-respect. It explains why progress felt difficult even with effort. It shows that repetition was not failure, but conditioning. And it opens the door to sustainable change—not through pressure, but through clarity.

When beliefs are examined, decisions regain freedom. When freedom returns, financial growth becomes possible—not as a struggle, but as a natural extension of new understanding.

Replacing False Beliefs with Grounded Financial Truths

False financial beliefs do not disappear when they are aggressively challenged. They disappear when they are outgrown. Most false beliefs were not created out of ignorance or weakness—they were formed as interpretations of lived experience. At one time, they helped a person make sense of uncertainty, instability, or disappointment. The problem is not that these beliefs existed; the problem is that they were never updated when life changed.

Replacing false beliefs begins with understanding what makes a belief "false." A false belief is not necessarily untrue in every circumstance. It is false because it is absolute, outdated, or incomplete. It takes a limited experience and turns it into a permanent rule. Statements like *"money never lasts," "I'm bad with money,"* or *"financial stability isn't for people like me"* feel convincing because they are familiar, not because they accurately describe reality.

Grounded financial truths work differently. They are not emotional conclusions. They are principles that hold across situations. They do not promise ease or perfection. They explain cause and effect. They feel steady rather than dramatic. And most importantly, they can be tested and observed in real life.

For example, the false belief *"money always disappears"* is replaced not with *"money always flows to me,"* but with the grounded truth *"money stays where there is structure, awareness, and consistency."* This truth removes emotion and introduces responsibility without blame. It explains past outcomes without condemning the person.

This distinction matters because the mind resists beliefs that feel unrealistic. If a new belief feels exaggerated or disconnected from experience, the nervous system rejects it. This is why many people fail when they try to replace scarcity thinking with overly optimistic affirmations. The mind knows when it is being pressured into pretending.

Grounded truths feel believable because they reflect how money actually behaves.

Another example: the belief *"I'm bad with money"* is not replaced with *"I'm amazing with money,"* but with *"financial skill is learned, practiced, and improved over time."* This truth restores agency without demanding perfection. It reframes mistakes as part of learning rather than evidence of identity.

Replacing false beliefs also requires slowing down automatic reactions. False beliefs operate quickly. They interpret situations instantly and trigger emotion. Grounded truths operate more slowly. They require pause, reflection, and repetition. This is why belief change feels awkward at first. The old belief is familiar; the new truth is still being learned.

The process often follows this pattern:

First, awareness. The person notices a recurring thought or reaction around money.

Second, interruption. They question the belief rather than automatically obey it.

Third, replacement. They introduce a grounded truth that better explains the situation.

Fourth, reinforcement. They act in alignment with the new truth, even in small ways.

Over time, repetition builds trust.

Importantly, replacing false beliefs does not mean suppressing old ones. Suppression creates resistance. Instead, the old belief is acknowledged: *"This belief made sense when I didn't have stability."* Then it is gently retired: *"But it no longer describes my reality or my capacity."*

This approach keeps the nervous system calm. It signals safety rather than threat. And safety is what allows beliefs to change.

Another essential element of grounded financial truths is neutrality. Grounded truths are not tied to self-worth. They separate behavior from identity. Instead of *"I failed,"* the truth becomes *"This strategy didn't work; I need to adjust."* This keeps learning active and shame low.

Grounded truths also support consistency. Because they are not emotionally extreme, they remain usable during stress. A belief that only works when everything is going well is fragile. A principle that holds under pressure is powerful.

Over time, acting from grounded truths reshapes experience. New experiences weaken old beliefs naturally. The mind stops expecting failure because it begins to observe stability. The emotional charge around money softens. Decisions feel less reactive. What once required effort begins to feel normal.

This is the real goal of belief replacement—not motivation, but alignment. When beliefs align with reality, behavior aligns with intention. There is no internal fight. Progress feels steadier and more sustainable.

Replacing false beliefs with grounded financial truths is not about becoming optimistic. It is about becoming accurate. It is about trading inherited assumptions for chosen understanding. And when understanding guides behavior, financial growth no longer feels like self-betrayal—it feels like self-respect.

Building a Healthier Money Identity

A money identity is not something people consciously choose. It is something they absorb over time. It forms through experience, repetition, feedback, and emotional association. Long before a person understands budgeting or investing, they already carry an internal sense of *who they are in relation to money*. That sense quietly guides every financial decision they make.

When someone says, *"I'm not good with money,"* they are not describing a skill gap—they are expressing an identity. And identity is powerful. It tells the mind which behaviors feel natural, which actions feel foreign, and which outcomes feel believable. This is why changing financial habits without addressing identity often fails. Habits can be forced temporarily. Identity cannot.

A healthier money identity begins with separating who you are from what you have experienced. Many people mistake repeated financial difficulty for proof of incapability. Over time, struggle becomes personal. The person stops saying, *"I struggled financially,"* and starts believing, *"I am someone who struggles financially."* This subtle shift changes everything.

Building a healthier identity does not require denying the past. It requires reframing its meaning. Past financial challenges were not evidence of incompetence; they were evidence of missing knowledge, unstable conditions, emotional pressure, or unexamined beliefs. When the past is reinterpreted accurately, it loses its power to define the future.

A healthy money identity is grounded, not inflated. It does not say, *"I'm great with money,"* when that feels untrue. It says, *"I am learning to handle money with awareness and consistency."* This identity is realistic, stable, and expandable. It allows growth without demanding perfection.

One of the most important shifts in building this identity is moving from judgment to stewardship. Judgment asks, *"What does this say about me?"* Stewardship asks, *"What does this need right now?"* When money is approached as something to manage rather than something that defines worth, decisions become calmer. Mistakes become feedback. Progress becomes something to maintain rather than prove.

A healthier money identity also includes emotional neutrality. Money stops being a source of shame or pride and becomes information. Numbers are no longer verdicts; they are data. This neutrality creates safety. And safety is what allows consistency. When a person does not feel attacked by their finances, they are more willing to engage with them honestly.

Another key element is identity expansion. A person does not replace an old identity by rejecting it; they outgrow it by adding new experiences. Each small act of consistency—tracking spending, pausing before a purchase, saving modestly, making a thoughtful decision—adds evidence. Over time, the mind updates its self-image: *"I am someone who pays attention." "I am someone who follows through." "I am someone who can be trusted with money."*

These identities are built through action, not affirmation. Repeated experience reshapes self-perception more effectively than words alone. This is why the book emphasizes small, sustainable shifts rather than dramatic change. Identity responds to proof.

A healthy money identity also distinguishes between income and worth. The person no longer measures themselves by how much they earn or have. Instead, they measure themselves by how intentionally they manage what passes through their hands. This creates dignity at every income level. Progress becomes internal as well as external.

Importantly, building a healthier money identity takes patience. Identity resists sudden change because it is tied to safety and familiarity. Old identities may resurface during stress. This is not failure—it is habit memory. Each time the person responds with awareness instead of self-attack, the new identity strengthens.

Over time, the relationship with money shifts. Money no longer feels like an examiner waiting to judge performance. It feels like a responsibility that can be handled steadily. The person no longer needs to prove their financial worth. They practice being someone who relates to money with clarity and respect.

This is the essence of a healthy money identity: not confidence rooted in numbers, not worth measured by income, but trust built through consistency and understanding.

When identity changes, behavior follows naturally. When behavior aligns, stability becomes sustainable. And when stability is sustained, financial freedom stops feeling distant and starts feeling possible.

CHAPTER 5

Discipline, Responsibility, and Financial Maturity

Discipline and responsibility are often misunderstood in the context of money. They are frequently framed as harsh traits—self-denial, rigidity, or relentless control. Many people resist them because they associate discipline with deprivation and responsibility with blame. This chapter exists to redefine these concepts in a healthier, more realistic way and to show that financial maturity is not about restriction, but about readiness.

Financial maturity begins when a person stops seeing money as something that happens *to* them and starts seeing it as something they actively steward. This shift does not occur through willpower alone. It happens when understanding, identity, and belief have already been rebuilt—as the earlier chapters have done. Only then can discipline become sustainable rather than exhausting.

Discipline, in its truest sense, is not force. It is alignment. It is the ability to act in ways that support long-term stability, even when short-term emotions pull in another direction. When discipline is rooted in fear or shame, it feels heavy and brittle. When it is rooted in clarity and self-respect, it feels calm and empowering.

This chapter helps the reader understand that most discipline failures are not moral failures—they are capacity failures. A person who is overwhelmed, anxious, or operating in survival mode does not lack discipline; they lack internal space. Expecting consistent discipline without emotional safety is unrealistic. Financial maturity requires the nervous system to feel steady enough to choose patience over urgency.

Responsibility is also reframed here. Responsibility does not mean blaming oneself for past mistakes or carrying guilt endlessly. True responsibility means responding appropriately to reality as it is now. It is forward-facing, not backward-punishing. A financially mature person acknowledges their current situation honestly, without drama or self-attack, and takes ownership of the next step—however small.

This chapter emphasizes that responsibility grows when shame decreases. When a person no longer feels judged by their finances, they are more willing to engage with them. Avoidance fades. Decisions become clearer. Responsibility becomes something they step into willingly, rather than something they are forced to accept.

Financial maturity also involves understanding trade-offs. Every financial decision consists of a choice between now and later, between comfort and stability, between ease and growth. A mature financial mindset does not eliminate desire—it contextualizes it. Instead of asking, *"Can I afford this?"* the question becomes, *"What does this choice cost me elsewhere?"* This shift reflects wisdom, not deprivation.

Another key aspect of financial maturity is consistency. Immature financial behavior is often reactive—driven by mood, stress, or external pressure. Mature financial behavior is steady. It does not require perfection. It requires follow-through. Small, repeated actions matter more than dramatic changes. This chapter helps the reader let go of the idea that financial growth must be fast to be valid.

Discipline in this context is also flexible. Financial maturity understands that life is dynamic. Plans adjust. Mistakes happen. What matters is the ability to return to intention without collapse or self-judgment. Rigidity is not maturity—resilience is.

The chapter also explores how financial maturity affects self-trust. Each time a person follows through on a small commitment—tracking spending, saving modestly, pausing before a purchase—they send a message to themselves: *I can be trusted.* Over time, this trust becomes internal stability. Discipline no longer feels like effort; it feels like identity in action.

Importantly, financial maturity does not mean having everything figured out. It means being willing to learn, to ask questions, and to make informed adjustments. A mature financial mindset replaces ego with curiosity. It allows growth without embarrassment.

By the end of this chapter, the reader understands that discipline is not punishment, responsibility is not blame, and maturity is not perfection. All three are expressions of respect—for time, for effort, and for future self.

This chapter marks a shift from internal reconstruction to practical readiness. The reader is no longer just understanding money differently—they are becoming someone who can hold, manage, and grow money sustainably.

Financial maturity is not about being strict. It is about being steady. It is not about denying life. It is about designing it intentionally.

And once discipline and responsibility are rooted in self-respect rather than fear, financial progress stops feeling like a struggle. It becomes a natural extension of who the reader has become.

Life Principles That Protect Wealth

Wealth is far easier to create than it is to protect. Many people focus intensely on earning, hustling, or accumulating, yet lose what they build because the inner and outer principles required to sustain wealth were never established. This chapter concept exists to shift the reader's focus from *how to get money* to *how to live in a way that allows money to stay, grow, and serve life well*.

At its core, wealth protection is not financial—it is behavioral, psychological, and ethical.

One of the most important life principles that protects wealth is clarity. Clarity means knowing what money is for. When money has no clear purpose, it is easily misused, drained, or sacrificed to impulse. People who lose wealth often do not do so because they are reckless, but because they lack. When money is not anchored to values, it becomes vulnerable to pressure, emotion, and distraction.

Clarity protects wealth by giving money direction. When a person knows what they are building toward—stability, freedom, security, legacy—decisions become easier.

Spending is evaluated through alignment, not emotion. Wealth stops being reactive and becomes intentional.

Another essential principle is self-regulation. Wealth amplifies who a person already is. If someone struggles with impulse, avoidance, or emotional decision-making, money magnifies those tendencies. Self-regulation is the ability to pause, reflect, and choose intentionally rather than reactively. It protects wealth by preventing decisions from being made under stress, excitement, fear, or ego.

Self-regulation is not suppression. It is awareness. It allows enjoyment without excess, ambition without recklessness, and generosity without self-sabotage. Without this principle, wealth becomes unstable, constantly responding to mood rather than wisdom.

Boundaries are another powerful protector of wealth. Boundaries are not selfish; they are structural. They define what money is responsible for—and what it is not. Without boundaries, money is pulled in many directions: supporting others beyond capacity, funding lifestyles that outpace income, or compensating for emotional discomfort. Wealth drains when money is used to solve problems it was never meant to fix.

Healthy boundaries protect wealth by ensuring that money serves a purpose rather than pressure. They allow generosity without resentment and support without collapse. Boundaries also protect against external influence—unsolicited advice, comparison, or expectations that do not align with the person's reality.

A crucial but often overlooked principle is humility. Wealth is fragile when ego leads decision-making. Humility allows a person to keep learning, seek counsel, and adjust course without defensiveness. It prevents overconfidence, risky shortcuts, and the belief that success guarantees immunity from error.

Humility protects wealth by keeping curiosity alive. It allows the person to say, *"I don't know everything,"* even in the face of success. This openness prevents stagnation and costly mistakes driven by pride.

Another life principle that protects wealth is consistency over intensity. Many people build wealth through bursts of effort but lose it through inconsistency. Financial maturity values steady habits more than dramatic actions. Small, repeated decisions—tracking, saving, reviewing, adjusting—create durability. Intensity may create momentum, but consistency creates sustainability.

This principle protects wealth by removing the need for motivation. Wealth that relies on constant excitement or pressure is unstable. Wealth supported by routine and rhythm is resilient.

Emotional neutrality around money is also critical. When cash becomes tied to identity, validation, or emotional regulation, it becomes volatile. Emotional neutrality allows money to be managed calmly. Gains do not inflate ego. Losses do not collapse self-worth. Decisions are made from clarity rather than reaction.

This principle protects wealth by preventing emotional extremes—both reckless optimism and paralyzing fear. It keeps money in its proper role: a tool, not a judge or rescuer.

Another foundational principle is long-term thinking. Wealth is rarely destroyed by one decision; it erodes through repeated short-term choices that ignore future consequences. Long-term thinking does not eliminate enjoyment—it contextualizes it. It asks, *"How does this decision affect tomorrow?"* before committing to today.

This principle protects wealth by aligning present behavior with future stability. It reduces regret, prevents the accumulation of hidden costs, and supports planning that outlasts momentary desire.

Finally, self-respect is a quiet but powerful protector of wealth. Self-respect shows up as honoring commitments, following through, and refusing to sabotage one's own progress. A person who respects themselves does not use money to escape discomfort or prove worth. They use it to support a life they value.

Self-respect creates internal accountability. It does not rely on fear or punishment. It sustains wealth because the person does not abandon themselves when choices become uncomfortable.

Together, these life principles form a protective framework. Money placed inside this framework becomes durable. Without it, even large sums are vulnerable.

This chapter teaches the reader a critical truth: Wealth is protected not by how much you have, but by who you are while you have it.

When clarity guides decisions, when self-regulation steadies behavior, when boundaries define responsibility, when humility keeps learning alive, when consistency replaces impulse, and when self-respect anchors identity, wealth stops slipping through the cracks.

It settles. It grows. And it begins to serve the life it was meant to support—not control.

This understanding prepares the reader for the next stage of the journey: learning how to build, manage, and sustain wealth in real-world conditions, with inner stability strong enough to carry outer success.

Why Discipline Is Protection, Not Punishment

For many people, the word *discipline* immediately triggers resistance. It brings images of restriction, deprivation, rigidity, and self-denial. Discipline is often associated with punishment—something imposed when a person is flawed, weak, or untrustworthy. This misunderstanding is one of the main reasons people struggle to sustain financial growth.

But discipline, in its true form, is not punishment. Discipline is protection.

Punishment is reactive. Protection is intentional. Punishment looks backward. Protection looks forward. Punishment shames. Protection preserves.

When discipline is misunderstood as punishment, it feels harsh and oppressive. People obey it temporarily, then rebel. They follow rules until exhaustion sets in, then abandon them entirely. This cycle creates guilt, frustration, and self-doubt. Not because discipline is harmful—but because it was framed incorrectly.

True discipline is not about denying yourself joy. It is about guarding your future self from unnecessary harm.

At its core, discipline exists to protect what matters. Just as boundaries protect relationships and structure protects buildings, discipline protects time, energy, peace, and financial stability. Without discipline, these things are exposed to impulse, pressure, emotion, and external demands.

Financial discipline, for example, is not about saying "no" to everything you want. It is about saying "yes" to what you don't want to lose. It protects you from decisions made in moments of stress, excitement, fear, or comparison—moments that often cost more than they give.

When a person lacks discipline, it is not because they enjoy chaos. It is usually because discipline has been framed as self-denial rather than self-respect. The mind resists what feels like punishment. It naturally avoids systems that feel harsh, controlling, or shame-based.

But when discipline is reframed as protection, the relationship changes.

Protection feels caring. Protection feels stabilizing. Protection feels aligned with self-respect.

A disciplined financial decision is not saying, *"I don't deserve this."* It is saying, *"I deserve stability more than momentary relief."*

This shift is subtle, but powerful.

Discipline also protects emotional well-being. Many financial mistakes are not caused by ignorance, but by emotional overwhelm. Discipline provides a pause between feeling and action. It gives space to breathe, evaluate, and choose intentionally rather than reactively. That pause is protective. It prevents regret, shame, and self-sabotage.

Importantly, discipline does not require perfection. Protection is not rigid—it is responsive. A financially mature discipline allows flexibility without collapse. When life happens, plans adjust. When mistakes occur, learning replaces punishment. The goal is not flawless behavior, but consistent care.

This is why discipline grows naturally when self-trust grows. Each time a person follows through on a small commitment, they prove to themselves that they can be trusted. That trust becomes internal safety, and where there is safety, discipline no longer feels forced.

Another critical insight is this: Discipline is what allows freedom to last.

Without discipline, freedom is fragile. Money comes in and leaves quickly. Progress starts and stops. Relief is temporary. With discipline, freedom becomes sustainable. Choices expand. Stress reduces. Stability increases.

Punishment restricts behavior out of fear. Protection guides behavior out of wisdom. When discipline is rooted in punishment, it sounds like:

- "I must control myself."
- "I can't be trusted."
- "I need to be stricter."

When discipline is rooted in protection, it sounds like:

- "I'm safeguarding my future."
- "I respect what I'm building."
- "I'm choosing what supports me."

This chapter's concept helps readers release internal resistance to discipline by showing that discipline is not something done *to* them—it is something done *for* them.

It is an act of care. An act of foresight. An act of maturity.

Discipline protects you from:

- Repeating emotional decisions
- Undoing progress you worked hard for
- Living in constant financial recovery mode

It creates a container strong enough to hold growth.

Once discipline is understood as protection, it stops feeling like pressure and becomes a sense of peace. It becomes the quiet structure that supports freedom, not the force that limits it.

And from that place, financial maturity stops being a struggle. It becomes a natural expression of self-respect and long-term care.

That is why discipline is not punishment. It is protection in its most practical form.

Responsibility as Freedom, Not Burden

Responsibility is often misunderstood as weight. Many people associate it with pressure, obligation, sacrifice, and loss of ease. To them, responsibility feels like something that limits life rather than expands it. This misunderstanding causes people to resist responsibility—especially financial responsibility—because it appears to demand more effort, more seriousness, and less enjoyment.

But true responsibility does not imprison. It liberates.

The feeling of responsibility as a burden usually comes from one of two places: blame or overwhelm. When responsibility is framed as *fault*—"this is my problem because I failed"—it feels heavy and shame-filled. When it is framed as *too much*—"everything depends on me"—it feels exhausting and unfair. In both cases, responsibility becomes something to avoid rather than embrace.

Freedom, however, does not come from avoiding responsibility. It comes from owning what you can control. Responsibility, in its healthiest form, means the ability to respond. It is not about carrying the past. It is about directing the present. A responsible person is not someone who has never made mistakes; it is someone who recognizes where their choices still matter and acts from that awareness.

When responsibility is avoided, life feels chaotic. Money feels unpredictable. Outcomes feel random. The person feels at the mercy of circumstances, timing, or other people's decisions. This state may appear easier in the short term, but it creates long-term anxiety. Lack of responsibility does not remove pressure—it removes power.

Taking responsibility restores power.

When someone says, *"This is my responsibility,"* they are not saying, *"This is my fault."* They are saying, *"This is within my influence."* That distinction changes everything.

In finances, responsibility brings clarity. Instead of feeling confused or reactive, the person knows where they stand. Numbers stop being threats and start being information. Decisions stop feeling forced and start feeling chosen. Even when resources are limited, responsibility provides a sense of direction. Direction creates calm. Calm creates freedom.

Responsibility also reduces mental load. When responsibility is avoided, the mind is constantly juggling uncertainty—what if something goes wrong, what if I should be doing more, what if I mess this up later. When responsibility is accepted, many of those "what ifs" dissolve. The person knows what they are handling and what they are not. Boundaries become clearer. Energy becomes focused.

Another reason responsibility feels like freedom is that it removes dependence. When a person takes responsibility for their financial life, they no longer wait for rescue—more income, better timing, someone else's support—to feel okay. They may still desire improvement, but they are no longer helpless in the present. This self-reliance creates dignity and confidence.

Importantly, responsibility does not mean doing everything alone. It means being honest about what you can manage and seeking help where appropriate. A mature sense of responsibility includes delegation, learning, and collaboration. Burden comes from believing you must carry everything. Freedom comes from knowing what is truly yours to take.

Responsibility also creates consistency. When actions are taken because they are chosen—not forced—follow-through becomes easier. Discipline becomes lighter. Habits stabilize—progress compounds. Over time, this consistency builds trust in oneself. And self-trust is one of the greatest forms of freedom a person can have.

When responsibility is rejected, freedom becomes fragile. It depends on circumstances staying favorable. When responsibility is embraced, freedom becomes resilient. It exists even when conditions are imperfect.

This concept also reframes adulthood and maturity. Financial maturity is not about restriction; it is about self-leadership. It is the moment a person realizes they can guide their life rather than react to it. That realization is empowering, not oppressive.

Responsibility as freedom sounds like:

- "I can influence this."
- "I have choices here."
- "I can respond intentionally."

- "I don't need to be perfect to be in charge."

Responsibility as burden sounds like:

- "This shouldn't be on me."
- "I'm failing if this is hard."
- "I can't handle this."
- "I'm trapped."

This chapter concept helps the reader shift from the second voice to the first.

When responsibility is understood correctly, it becomes grounding. It anchors a person in reality without shame. It allows them to build steadily rather than hope desperately. It turns financial management into self-respect in action.

Ultimately, responsibility is freedom because it returns agency to the individual. It says, "I am not powerless here." And that realization—quiet, steady, and practical—is what makes lasting financial stability possible.

Responsibility does not take life away. It gives life direction. And direction is what turns effort into progress, and progress into peace.

Consistency Over Intensity in Money Habits

Many people approach money with intensity. They overhaul everything at once, create strict rules, set ambitious targets, and promise themselves that *this time* they will do it perfectly. For a short while, it works. Motivation is high. Control feels strong. Progress appears fast. Then life happens.

Energy drops. Stress rises. One missed action becomes two. The system feels fragile. Guilt creeps in. Eventually, the entire effort collapses—not because the person is incapable, but because intensity is not designed to last.

Consistency is the quiet, often uncelebrated habit of doing the right thing *most of the time*, even when motivation is low and circumstances are imperfect. It does not rely on emotional drive. It depends on rhythm. And rhythm is what builds financial stability.

Intensity focuses on how much you do in a short period. Consistency focuses on how often you do something over time.

Money responds far better to the second.

When habits are built with intensity, they depend on mood, discipline, and willpower. When habits are built with consistency, they rely on structure and repetition. Willpower fluctuates. Structure remains. This is why consistent habits survive stress, while intense ones often fail under it.

Consider saving. Many people wait for the "right moment" to save a large amount. They push themselves to save aggressively, then stop entirely when the pressure becomes uncomfortable. This pattern creates start-and-stop progress. Savings grow, then disappear. Emotion drives the process.

Consistency reframes saving as a non-dramatic behavior. Small, regular contributions—even when they feel insignificant—build momentum and trust. Over time, consistency compounds. What intensity could not hold, consistency stabilizes.

The same is true for spending. Intense approaches often involve strict bans, complete deprivation, or rigid rules. These methods create tension. Eventually, tension seeks release—often through impulsive spending that undoes progress. The person feels like they "failed," when in reality, the system was unsustainable.

Consistent spending habits focus on awareness rather than control. Instead of forbidding everything, they encourage pausing, choosing, and adjusting. A consistent habit might be as simple as reviewing spending weekly or checking in before larger purchases. These small actions prevent damage without creating rebellion. Consistency also protects earning growth. Intensity may manifest as overwork, burnout, or the pursuit of quick wins. This can lead to temporary income increases followed by exhaustion or instability. Consistent earning growth prioritizes skill development, steady improvement, and repeatable systems. It builds income that lasts rather than spikes that disappear.

Another reason consistency matters is the formation of identity. Identity is shaped by repeated behavior, not occasional effort. A person does not become "someone who handles money well" in one intense month. They become that person by months and years of showing up calmly and reliably. Each small act of consistency reinforces self-trust: *I do what I say I will do.*

Intensity often ties progress to self-worth. When performance drops, shame follows. Consistency separates worth from outcome. Missing one day does not mean failure—it simply means returning the next day. This creates a sense of emotional safety, which is essential for long-term change.

Consistency also aligns with how the nervous system works. Intense financial changes can trigger fear, resistance, or overwhelm. The mind interprets sudden restriction as a threat. Consistent changes, however, feel manageable. They allow the nervous system to adapt gradually. This is why consistent habits feel boring—but boring is stable. And stability is powerful.

Importantly, consistency does not mean minimal effort forever. It means right-sized effort sustained over time—small actions compound. Systems strengthen. Capacity grows. What once felt difficult becomes normal. Over time, consistency naturally creates intensity—without burnout.

This principle also protects against self-sabotage. Intensity raises expectations quickly. When reality doesn't keep up, disappointment sets in. Consistency keeps expectations realistic. Progress feels earned rather than forced. The urge to quit diminishes because the system is not punishing.

Consistency over intensity is ultimately a principle of respect—respect for your energy, your life, and your future self. It acknowledges that you are human, not a machine. It builds systems that support you even on hard days.

In money habits, consistency looks like:

- Small, regular savings instead of rare, large deposits
- Ongoing awareness instead of occasional strict control

- Steady learning instead of dramatic overhauls
- Returning to the plan instead of abandoning it

Intensity may impress temporarily. Consistency changes outcomes permanently.

When money habits are built on consistency, progress becomes durable. Financial stability stops being something you chase and becomes something you *maintain*. And maintenance—not motivation—is what creates lasting freedom.

This concept anchors financial maturity in realism. It reminds the reader that wealth is not built by heroic effort, but by reliable behavior repeated patiently.

That is why consistency, not intensity, is the habit that truly transforms financial life.

Learning to Manage Small Amounts with Care

One of the most overlooked truths about money is that how a person treats small amounts is how they will treat large ones. This is not a moral statement—it is a practical one. Money does not change behavior; it amplifies it. The habits formed at a small scale are the same habits that operate at a larger scale, just with greater consequences.

Many people believe they will become careful, disciplined, or intentional *after* they have more money. They see their current situation as temporary and therefore undeserving of serious attention. Small amounts feel insignificant, almost invisible. But this mindset quietly delays growth, because capacity is built before increase, not after.

Managing small amounts with care is not about limitation. It is about readiness.

Small amounts reveal patterns clearly. When resources are limited, every decision matters more. Spending choices, saving behavior, and priorities are easier to observe because the margin for error is small. This makes small amounts the most honest training ground for financial maturity. They show where money leaks, where emotion overrides intention, and where structure is missing.

When a person dismisses small amounts as "not enough to matter," they unintentionally practice disengagement. They stop tracking. They stop planning. They stop reflecting. Over time, this creates a habit of carelessness—not because the person lacks character, but because the system was never taken seriously. When more money arrives, that habit remains.

Caring for small amounts teaches attention. Attention is the core skill behind all money management. It is the ability to notice where money goes, why it is used, and what it is supporting. Without attention, money becomes reactive. With attention, money becomes intentional. This skill is transferable regardless of income level.

Managing small amounts also teaches respect. Respect does not mean fear or obsession. It means acknowledging that every resource—no matter how small—represents time, effort, and opportunity. When a person treats little money with respect, they communicate to themselves: *I take my financial life seriously, even before it looks impressive.*

This self-message is powerful. Identity follows behavior.

Another critical reason this concept matters is that small amounts are emotionally safer to practice with. Mistakes made at a small scale are less costly and more forgiving. This allows learning without overwhelming consequences. A person can experiment, adjust, and improve without fear of major loss. Avoiding this learning stage only delays growth and increases risk later.

Caring for small amounts also builds consistency. Saving a modest amount regularly, tracking simple expenses, or pausing before everyday purchases creates rhythm.

Rhythm stabilizes behavior. Over time, these rhythms become automatic. When income grows, the system expands naturally rather than collapsing under pressure.

This principle also addresses entitlement thinking. Some people unconsciously believe they will "deserve" discipline or structure only after reaching a certain financial level. In reality, discipline and structure are what make higher levels sustainable. Money grows into systems—it does not create them.

Managing small amounts with care also reshapes emotional relationships with money. It reduces anxiety because awareness replaces uncertainty. It builds confidence because follow-through replaces doubt. The person begins to trust themselves—not because they have more, but because they handle what they have well.

Importantly, this concept removes shame from starting small. There is no humiliation in small beginnings. There is wisdom in preparation. Small stewardship is not a sign of lack; it is a sign of maturity in formation.

When a person learns to manage small amounts with care:

- Spending becomes more thoughtful
- Saving becomes more consistent

- Decisions become calmer
- Progress becomes predictable

This principle creates stability before expansion. It ensures that when opportunity arrives—higher income, larger responsibility, greater access—the person is ready to hold it.

Ultimately, learning to manage small amounts with care is about becoming trustworthy with resources. Trust is not given by income level; it is earned through behavior.

Money responds to stewardship. Growth responds to readiness. And readiness is built quietly, patiently, and deliberately—starting exactly where a person is.

That is why this concept is not about the size of the money. It is about character, awareness, and preparation.

And those qualities, once formed, scale effortlessly.

CHAPTER 6

Preparing Your Life for Financial Increase

Financial increase does not begin with more money. It starts with capacity. Capacity is the ability to receive, manage, and sustain an increase without chaos, fear, or self-sabotage. Many people focus on attracting more income without realizing that their current life structure cannot support it. When an increase arrives without preparation, it often creates stress, instability, or loss rather than freedom.

This chapter exists to address a critical truth: money grows into systems, not intentions.

Preparing your life for financial increase means ensuring that your inner world, daily habits, responsibilities, and environment are aligned with growth. Without this alignment, more money does not solve problems—it exposes them.

The first area of preparation is mental readiness. Increase requires a mind that can tolerate expansion without panic. When someone has lived in survival mode for a long time, stability itself can feel unfamiliar. More money brings new decisions, new responsibilities, and new expectations. If the mind is still operating from scarcity, increase can trigger anxiety rather than relief. Preparing mentally means developing calm, clarity, and confidence before the numbers change.

This chapter reinforces that a prepared mind views increase as something to steward, not something to cling to or fear losing. It is no longer asking, *"What if this disappears?"* but *"How do I manage this wisely?"*

The second area of preparation is emotional capacity. Money amplifies emotion. If a person is already overwhelmed, stressed, or emotionally reactive, more money magnifies those states. Emotional preparation means learning to regulate feelings around success, pressure, comparison, and responsibility. It means experiencing progress without guilt, fear, or the urge to self-sabotage.

Financial increase requires emotional steadiness—the ability to stay grounded during change. This steadiness is built through awareness, not avoidance.

The third area is life structure. Structure includes routines, systems, boundaries, and organization. A life without structure leaks energy, time, and money. Increase, entering an unstructured life quickly gets consumed by chaos—unexpected expenses, disorganization, poor planning, and reactive decisions.

Preparing your life structurally means building simple, repeatable systems before income grows. This includes:

- Clear routines for managing money
- Basic planning habits
- Boundaries around time and obligations
- An order in daily life that reduces decision fatigue

Structure creates containment. It gives money somewhere to land.

Another essential aspect of preparation is responsibility alignment. Many people desire more money without considering what it will require of them. Increase often demands better decision-making, stronger boundaries, clearer priorities, and greater follow-through. If someone resents responsibility, they may unconsciously resist increases because they feel like added pressure.

This chapter reframes responsibility as freedom, showing that accepting appropriate responsibility before increase actually reduces stress later. A prepared life has clarity about what the person is responsible for—and what they are not.

Preparing for an increase also means gently upgrading self-expectations. This is not about perfection or pressure. It is about asking honest questions:

- Can I consistently manage what I already have?
- Do I follow through on small commitments?
- Is my current lifestyle aligned with growth or constant recovery?

These questions are not judgments—they are diagnostics. They reveal readiness.

Another critical area is environmental alignment. The environment includes physical space, relationships, and influences. Financial growth is difficult to sustain in environments that constantly drain energy, encourage comparison, or normalize instability. Preparation may involve simplifying surroundings, setting boundaries with people, or reducing exposure to financial noise and pressure.

A supportive environment does not guarantee success, but a draining one almost guarantees struggle.

This chapter also addresses timing. Financial increase often comes gradually, not suddenly. Preparation allows a person to grow with the increase rather than be overwhelmed by it. Instead of waiting for a dramatic breakthrough, the reader learns to expand capacity step by step, matching growth with readiness.

One of the most important lessons in this chapter is that preparation is invisible but powerful. No one applauds the systems you build before success. No one celebrates the discipline you practice before increase. But these unseen preparations determine whether success becomes stable or temporary.

By the end of this chapter, the reader understands that preparing for financial increase is not about being perfect, rich, or fearless. It is about being ready. Ready to hold more without losing peace. Prepared to manage more without losing clarity. Ready to grow without losing self-respect.

This chapter marks a shift from internal maturity to external readiness. The reader is no longer just changing how they think—they are aligning their lives.

Financial increase is not a reward. It is a responsibility. And responsibility, when prepared for, becomes freedom.

When life is prepared, money becomes an asset rather than a disruption. When capacity is built, the increase becomes sustainable. And when preparation meets opportunity, growth finally has somewhere safe to stay.

Order Before Expansion

Expansion is attractive—more money, more opportunities, more freedom, more options. Many people focus their energy on expansion because it feels like progress. Order, on the other hand, feels ordinary. It feels slow, unexciting, and sometimes unnecessary—especially when resources already feel limited. Yet this is where many financial journeys break down.

Expansion without order does not create freedom. It creates pressure.

Order is the internal and external structure that allows growth to settle instead of scatter. It is not about perfection or control. It is about containment—having systems, clarity, and rhythm strong enough to hold what is coming.

When life lacks order, increase does not improve it. It exposes it.

Order begins internally. A person may want financial growth, but if their mind is disorganized—constantly anxious, reactive, or overwhelmed—more money intensifies that state. New decisions appear. New expectations arise—new risks surface. Without internal order, the mind struggles to prioritize, regulate emotion, and respond calmly. Expansion then feels stressful rather than empowering.

This is why people sometimes feel worse after financial improvement. The increase is real, but the internal capacity to manage it has not caught up.

Order also exists in daily life. This includes routines, time management, planning habits, and basic organization. A life that is already chaotic—missed deadlines, unmanaged obligations, unclear priorities—has no place for expansion to land. More money enters the same disorder and quickly disappears into it.

Order gives money direction.

Without order, money responds to urgency. With order, money responds to intention.

Another important aspect of order is decision clarity. In disordered systems, every decision feels urgent and exhausting. There is no framework to guide choices, so energy is drained constantly. Expansion multiplies decisions. Without order, decision fatigue sets in quickly, leading to more mistakes and stronger emotional reactions.

Order reduces noise. It simplifies choices. It allows a person to say, *"This is how I handle money,"* instead of reinventing the process every time.

Order is also relational. Relationships that lack boundaries, clarity, or mutual respect often become financial drains. When a person expands financially without relational order, pressure increases—expectations rise, requests multiply, and resentment can form. Order in relationships protects both money and peace.

Importantly, order does not mean rigidity. It means predictability. Predictability allows the nervous system to relax. When the nervous system is calm, growth feels safe. When growth feels safe, it can be sustained.

Expansion without order often leads to:

- Emotional overwhelm
- Impulsive decisions
- Self-sabotage
- Burnout
- Loss of progress

Order before expansion prevents these outcomes.

This principle applies universally. Businesses fail not because they expand, but because they develop faster than their systems. Relationships strain not because they grow, but because structure is missing. Personal finances collapse not because income increases, but because habits and clarity did not scale with it.

Order answers foundational questions:

- Where does money go?
- What am I responsible for?
- What comes first?
- What supports my future?

When these questions are unanswered, expansion feels dangerous. When they are answered, expansion feels natural.

Another key insight is that order creates trust. When you handle what you already have with clarity and consistency, you build confidence in yourself. That trust is internal safety, and safety is what allows expansion to be held without fear.

Many people believe order will come *after* success. In reality, success settles where order already exists. Order is not a reward—it is preparation.

This chapter concept teaches the reader to value the invisible work: organizing life, clarifying priorities, building systems, and creating rhythm. These actions rarely feel impressive, but they determine whether growth lasts.

Order before expansion means:

- Clarity before complexity
- Stability before scale
- Systems before speed
- Capacity before the increase

When order is present, expansion becomes steady instead of chaotic. Growth stops feeling like a threat and starts feeling like progress.

Order does not slow you down. It protects your momentum.

And when order leads, expansion follows in a way that strengthens life rather than overwhelms it.

Why Money Exposes Disorder

Money is often blamed for problems it did not create. People say money changed them, ruined relationships, or created chaos in their lives. In reality, money is not a creator of disorder—it is a revealer of it. Money exposes disorder by amplifying existing patterns, habits, and structures. What is already present beneath the surface becomes more visible when money enters the picture.

This is one of the most important truths in financial maturity: money does not fix disorder, and it does not create order—it highlights what is already there.

Disorder arises when clarity, structure, or alignment is lacking. This can appear internally—as confusion, emotional instability, or conflicting priorities—or externally—as disorganized routines, unmanaged responsibilities, and unclear systems. When money is limited, disorder may remain partially hidden because the margin for action is small. When cash increases, the margin expands, and so does visibility.

For example, someone who struggles with impulse under pressure may not notice it strongly when funds are tight. But when money increases, the impulse has room to act. The result looks like sudden overspending or poor choices, when in fact it is the same pattern operating at a larger scale.

Money also exposes emotional disorders. If a person uses money to regulate emotions—spending to soothe stress, earning to feel worthy, avoiding money to escape shame—these behaviors become more pronounced as resources increase. More money does not calm emotional patterns; it gives them more expression.

Another way money exposes disorder is through decision volume. Increase brings options. Options require clarity. Without clarity, decision-making becomes exhausting and error-prone. Choices are made reactively, influenced by mood, pressure, or comparison. What looks like irresponsibility is often simply an uncontained choice.

Money also exposes relational disorder. Relationships without boundaries become strained when money enters.

Expectations rise. Requests increase. Power dynamics shift. Unspoken assumptions surface. Money does not create these tensions—it reveals them. Without relational clarity, financial growth leads to conflict rather than cooperation.

Money further exposes disorder in values. When values are unclear, spending becomes erratic. One moment, money is saved aggressively; the next, it is spent impulsively. This inconsistency is not about discipline—it is about misalignment. Money highlights where values conflict or where priorities were never defined.

Time disorder is also revealed. People who are already overwhelmed by poor time management often find that financial growth adds stress rather than relief. More money does not create more time—it demands better use of the time it already provides. Without order, increased leads to burnout rather than freedom.

Importantly, money does not expose disorder to be punished—it exposes it to be addressed. Exposure is an invitation, not a judgment. When disorder is revealed, it shows exactly where growth is needed. It points to systems that need structure, habits that need adjustment, and boundaries that need strengthening.

This is why many people experience discomfort after financial improvement. The discomfort is not because money is bad. It is because cash removed the camouflage that limited the resources provided. The chaos was already there—money made it visible.

Understanding this changes the approach to financial growth. Instead of chasing more money as a solution, the focus shifts to creating order first. Order absorbs increase. Disorder repels it.

Order means:

- Clear priorities
- Simple systems
- Emotional regulation
- Healthy boundaries
- Aligned values

When order is present, money feels supportive. When it is absent, money feels overwhelming.

This concept also removes shame. If money exposes disorder, then financial struggle is not evidence of failure—it is feedback. Feedback shows where structure is missing. Structure can be built.

Money is not judging you. It is revealing your readiness.

When disorder is addressed, money behaves differently. It stops scattering and starts settling. Growth becomes sustainable because it has something to attach to.

This chapter concept prepares the reader for a critical shift: before asking for more, become stable with what you have. Not because you are undeserving—but because increase deserves a place where it can stay.

Money exposes disorder not to embarrass you, but to show you where to build.

And once you build order, money stops revealing chaos—and starts supporting expansion.

Identifying Financial Leaks and Weak Structures

Financial struggle is often described as a lack of money, but in reality, it is more frequently a loss of containment. Money enters, but it does not stay. It flows out quietly, steadily, and often invisibly. These losses are not always dramatic or reckless. They happen through small, repeated gaps—what we can call *financial leaks*—and through systems that were never strong enough to hold money in the first place—*weak structures*.

Identifying these leaks and weak structures is not about criticism. It is about clarity. Money does not disappear randomly. It follows pathways. When those pathways are unclear or unguarded, money moves through them.

A financial leak is any repeated outflow of money that does not meaningfully support stability, growth, or well-being. Leaks are rarely obvious at first glance. They hide in habits, routines, emotional patterns, and convenience choices. Because each leak feels small, it seldom triggers an alarm. But over time, their cumulative effect can be devastating.

Weak structures, on the other hand, are not about spending at all. They are about absence—the absence of systems, boundaries, and processes that intentionally guide money. Even a moderate income cannot last long without structure. Money needs direction, timing, and protection. Without these, it becomes reactive.

One of the most common leaks comes from unexamined daily spending. Small, frequent purchases made without awareness—subscriptions, convenience spending, impulse buys—rarely feel significant in isolation. But because they are habitual, they create a constant drain. The issue is not the spending itself; it is the lack of conscious choice. When money leaves without reflection, it leaves without alignment.

Another major leak comes from emotional compensation. Money is often used to regulate stress, exhaustion, or dissatisfaction. This spending does not feel indulgent; it feels necessary in the moment. Yet because it is driven by emotion rather than intention, it rarely delivers lasting relief. Over time, it creates a pattern where money is repeatedly exchanged for temporary comfort, leaving stability untouched.

Financial leaks also occur through poor timing. Paying late fees, missing discounts, making last-minute decisions, or failing to plan for predictable expenses all cost money unnecessarily. These losses are not caused by lack of income, but by lack of anticipation. Weak timing structures force cash to respond to urgency rather than to strategy.

Weak structures become clear in the absence of clear categories and priorities. When money has no defined purpose, every expense competes equally. Savings feel optional. Planning feels abstract. As a result, cash flows toward what is loudest or most urgent, not what is most important. Without structure, money does not reflect values—it reflects pressure.

Another weak structure is the lack of review. Money that is never reviewed cannot be adjusted. Many people avoid looking at their finances because it triggers anxiety or shame. But avoidance allows leaks to continue unnoticed. Review is not about control; it is about feedback. Without feedback, systems decay.

Relational dynamics can also create leaks. Supporting others beyond capacity, responding to unspoken expectations, or avoiding difficult financial conversations all lead to gradual depletion. These leaks are especially difficult to see because they are tied to care, loyalty, or fear of conflict. Without boundaries, money is asked to solve relational discomfort—and it cannot.

Weak earning structures also contribute. Inconsistent income, underpricing skills, lack of savings buffers, or dependence on a single fragile source all create vulnerability. When income lacks structure, money is always in recovery mode. Even good months are spent fixing the last bad one. This cycle prevents accumulation and reinforces scarcity.

Importantly, leaks and weak structures are not signs of irresponsibility. They are signs of missing systems. No one naturally manages money well without structure. Structure must be built deliberately.

Identifying leaks requires slowing down and observing patterns, not judging decisions. The key questions are not:

- "Why am I so bad with money?" But:
- "Where does money consistently leave?"
- "What decisions repeat?"
- "What expenses feel invisible?"
- "Where does urgency replace intention?"

Once identified, leaks lose their power. Awareness alone often reduces them. Weak structures, once named, can be strengthened gradually. A simple review habit, clearer categories, better timing, or firmer boundaries can seal gaps that previously drained resources.

This concept teaches a crucial truth: financial stability is less about how much you earn and more about how well you manage your money. Containment does not mean restriction. It means support. Money stays where it is guided, reviewed, and respected.

When leaks are sealed and structures are strengthened, money behaves differently. It accumulates. It rests. It grows.

Not because income changed—but because readiness did.

Identifying financial leaks and weak structures is not a one-time task. It is an ongoing practice of stewardship.

And each improvement, no matter how small, increases capacity for stability and growth.

This understanding prepares the reader for the next step: building systems strong enough to withstand financial growth without stress or loss.

Creating Simple Awareness Systems (Not Rigid Budgets)

For many people, the word *budget* triggers immediate resistance. It feels restrictive, judgmental, and fragile. Budgets often collapse not because people are irresponsible, but because the systems they try to follow demand perfection, emotional neutrality, and constant discipline—things real life rarely provides.

This chapter concept introduces a healthier alternative: awareness systems.

An awareness system is not designed to control money. It is designed to help you see clearly.

Clarity changes behavior naturally. Control tries to force it. Rigid budgets assume life is predictable. Awareness systems accept that life is dynamic. Instead of telling you exactly what you *must* do, they help you understand what you *are* doing—consistently, honestly, and without shame.

From that understanding, better decisions emerge organically.

The problem with rigid budgets is not structure—it is rigidity. When budgets are too detailed, too strict, or too moralized, they break under stress. One unexpected expense feels like failure. One emotional purchase feels like a collapse. The result is often abandonment: *"I couldn't stick to it, so I stopped."*

Awareness systems are built to survive imperfection.

At their core, awareness systems answer simple questions:

- Where is my money actually going?
- What patterns repeat?
- What feels aligned, and what feels draining?
- What decisions do I make automatically?

These systems work because behavior changes when it is observed. When spending is visible, it becomes intentional. When income is tracked gently, it becomes manageable. When patterns are named, they can be adjusted.

An awareness system does not require tracking every cent. It requires consistent check-ins. These check-ins might be weekly, bi-weekly, or monthly. The frequency matters less than the regularity. The goal is to create a habit of noticing, not a spreadsheet of perfection.

For example, instead of assigning strict spending limits, an awareness system might categorize expenses broadly—needs, wants, savings, obligations—and review how money flowed through those categories. This keeps the focus on direction rather than restriction.

Awareness systems also remove moral judgment. Money behavior is treated as data, not a verdict. There is no "good" or "bad" spending—only information. This reduces shame and defensiveness, which are the biggest blockers to consistency.

When people feel judged by their systems, they avoid them. When they are informed, they return.

Another strength of awareness systems is adaptability—especially to life changes. Income fluctuates. Priorities shift. Awareness systems can adjust without collapsing. Instead of breaking when conditions change, they respond. This makes them sustainable.

Awareness systems also reduce decision fatigue. When you regularly observe patterns, many decisions become easier. You already know where money tends to leak. You already know which expenses feel worth it. This reduces the mental load of constant evaluation.

Importantly, awareness systems support emotional regulation. Many financial decisions are made quickly to relieve stress or pressure. Awareness slows the process. It introduces a pause between impulse and action. That pause is often enough to change the outcome.

Another key advantage is self-trust. Each time you engage with your awareness system—without avoidance—you reinforce the identity of someone who pays attention. Over time, this builds confidence. Money stops feeling overwhelming because it is no longer invisible.

Awareness systems also scale. What works at a small income level works at a larger one. The same habit of review, reflection, and adjustment expands naturally with growth. Unlike rigid budgets, awareness systems do not need to be rebuilt every time income changes.

This approach reframes money management as relationship-building rather than rule-following. You are learning how money behaves in your life. You are learning how you respond to it. This knowledge is far more valuable than perfect compliance.

Creating simple awareness systems means:

- Observing patterns without judgment
- Reviewing money regularly without pressure
- Adjusting gently rather than enforcing harsh rules
- Building clarity instead of control

When awareness is present, discipline becomes easier. When clarity exists, structure forms naturally. When systems feel supportive, consistency follows.

This concept prepares the reader to manage money sustainably—without burnout, rebellion, or shame. It teaches that financial maturity is not about tightening control, but about strengthening understanding.

Money does not need to be policed. It needs to be seen. And once money is seen clearly, it can finally be guided wisely.

Signs You Are Becoming Financially Ready

Financial readiness is often misunderstood as a number—more income, a certain savings amount, or freedom from debt. In reality, financial readiness is a state of stability, awareness, and capacity. It shows up in how you think, feel, and decide long before it shows up in your bank balance.

The signs of readiness are usually subtle. They do not announce themselves with excitement or confidence. They appear as calm, consistency, and clarity. Many people overlook these signs because they expect readiness to feel like certainty. In truth, it feels like grounded competence.

One of the first signs of financial readiness is reduced emotional reactivity around money. Money no longer triggers immediate fear, excitement, shame, or avoidance. You can look at your finances—even when they are imperfect—without spiraling. This emotional steadiness is critical. It means decisions are no longer driven primarily by mood or pressure, but by understanding.

Another sign is increased awareness without obsession. You know where your money generally goes. You review it regularly. You notice patterns. But you are not consumed by tracking every detail. This balance shows maturity. Awareness is present, but anxiety is not in control.

Financial readiness also shows up as follow-through on small commitments. You do what you say you will do financially—most of the time. You save modestly. You pause before spending. You review when you plan to review. These actions may feel ordinary, but they are powerful. Follow-through builds self-trust, and self-trust is a prerequisite for handling more responsibility.

Another key sign is clarity about priorities. You are no longer equally pulled by every desire or expense. You know what matters most right now—stability, growth, learning, rest, or preparation—and your money generally reflects that. This does not mean perfection. It means alignment. Money starts to support your life instead of pulling it in multiple directions.

You may also notice fewer comparisons. Other people's financial choices, timelines, or successes feel less triggering. You are more focused on your own systems and progress. This indicates that your identity is no longer tied to external validation through money. Comparison fades when internal direction strengthens.

Financial readiness includes comfort with gradual progress. You no longer feel the need to rush, catch up, or force outcomes. You understand that stability is built over time. This patience is not passive—it is intentional. It allows you to make decisions that support sustainability rather than short-term relief.

Another sign is a healthier relationship with discipline. Discipline no longer feels like punishment or pressure. It feels protective. You choose boundaries and systems because they support you, not because you are afraid of failing. When discipline feels caring rather than harsh, readiness is present.

You may also notice a willingness to learn without embarrassment. You ask questions. You seek clarity. You adjust strategies. You no longer see learning as proof of inadequacy. This openness keeps growth alive and prevents stagnation.

Financial readiness also appears as acceptance of responsibility without overwhelm. You recognize what is within your control and take ownership of it calmly. You no longer feel crushed by responsibility or tempted to avoid it. Responsibility feels like agency, not burden.

Another important sign is reduced self-sabotage during progress. When things improve slightly, you do not immediately undo them. You allow gains to settle. You tolerate stability without creating drama. This is a powerful indicator of readiness, especially for those who have lived in survival mode.

You may also experience greater alignment between lifestyle and capacity. You make choices that fit your current reality rather than trying to perform a version of success you cannot yet sustain. This honesty protects progress and reduces financial strain.

Perhaps the most important sign is self-respect in financial decisions. You do not abandon yourself to please others, escape discomfort, or prove worth. You consider your future self. You make decisions you can stand behind—even when they are simple or modest.

None of these signs requires a high income. None requires perfection. All of them indicate readiness.

Financial readiness is not loud. It does not rush. It does not need validation. It feels like:

- Calm engagement instead of avoidance
- Awareness instead of anxiety
- Consistency instead of intensity
- Clarity instead of confusion

When these signs are present, the increase no longer destabilizes. It integrates. Growth becomes something you can hold, not just chase.

This concept reassures the reader that readiness is already forming—often quietly. It shifts the focus from waiting for a breakthrough to recognizing preparation in progress.

Financial increase does not arrive to make you ready. It comes because you are becoming prepared.

And readiness, once established, changes not just what you earn—but what you keep, grow, and sustain.

CHAPTER 7

Becoming Financially Ready

Becoming financially ready is not a moment. It is not a milestone. It is not something that happens *after* money arrives.

Financial readiness is a state of internal and external alignment—a quiet maturity that allows money to enter, settle, and grow without creating instability, fear, or self-sabotage. This chapter exists to help the reader recognize that readiness is something they *become*, not something they wait for.

Throughout this book, the focus has intentionally been placed on the inner life first: beliefs, emotions, identity, discipline, responsibility, order, and awareness. This is because money does not move independently of the person holding it. It moves through the systems of thought, behavior, and structure already in place.

Financial readiness occurs when those systems begin to work together.

At its core, becoming financially ready means that money no longer feels like an external force that controls your emotions or decisions. It feels like a responsibility you can handle—calmly, intentionally, and without panic. This does not require wealth. It requires capacity.

One of the clearest signs of financial readiness is stability in the face of imperfection. A financially ready person does not need everything to be ideal before they engage with money. They can plan even when income fluctuates. They can review finances even when mistakes exist. They do not wait for confidence to act—confidence grows because they act.

Readiness also shows up as integration. Earlier, money may have felt separate from life—something stressful, avoided, or emotionally charged. In preparedness, money becomes integrated into daily living. It is considered alongside time, energy, health, and values. Decisions feel connected rather than fragmented.

Another defining feature of readiness is self-leadership. A financially ready person does not outsource responsibility for their financial life to hope, luck, or rescue. They understand what is within their control and act there consistently. They no longer confuse lack of control over everything with lack of control over anything.

This does not mean they stop dreaming or aspiring. It means their aspirations are grounded in preparation rather than fantasy.

Financial readiness also includes emotional tolerance for growth. Growth brings change. Change brings discomfort. A ready person can tolerate the discomfort of improvement without retreating into old patterns. They allow progress to stabilize. They do not rush to spend, prove, or escape as soon as things improve.

This ability to *let improvement last* is one of the most overlooked forms of readiness.

Becoming financially ready also means that discipline, responsibility, and structure no longer feel like threats to freedom. They feel like supports. The reader no longer sees systems as cages, but as containers that protect peace and momentum. They understand that freedom without structure is fragile—and structure without self-respect is unsustainable.

Readiness also shows in realistic self-expectations. The financially ready person no longer demands perfection from themselves. They expect consistency, honesty, and adjustment. This makes follow-through possible. They build habits they can maintain, not standards they will eventually rebel against.

Another important element of readiness is respect for timing. The reader understands that growth unfolds in stages. They stop comparing their chapter one to someone else's chapter ten. This patience does not slow progress—it stabilizes it. Rushed growth often collapses. Prepared growth compounds.

Financial readiness also involves clean boundaries—with money, with people, and with oneself. The reader can say no without guilt, yes without self-betrayal, and pause without panic. Boundaries reduce leakage and resentment, allowing money to serve its intended purpose.

Perhaps most importantly, becoming financially ready means the reader has made peace with money. Money is no longer an enemy, a savior, or a measure of worth. It is a tool—powerful, neutral, and manageable. This peace creates clarity. Clarity creates consistency. Consistency creates stability.

By the end of this chapter, the reader understands a critical truth: Financial readiness is not about how much money you have. It is about how much responsibility, clarity, and stability you can hold without losing yourself.

This chapter does not promise immediate wealth. It promises something more valuable at this stage: preparedness. Preparedness ensures that when opportunity arrives—whether gradually or suddenly—it does not overwhelm. It settles. It stays. It grows.

This is why Book 1 ends here.

The reader is no longer operating from a place of lack, shame, or confusion. They are no longer chasing money to fix internal instability. They are becoming someone who can receive money without being undone by it.

From this place, the next phase becomes possible.

Book 2 will not need to convince the reader that wealth is possible. It will show them how to build it—because now, they are ready to hold it.

Financial readiness is not loud. It does not announce itself. It feels like calm competence. And calm competence is the foundation of lasting freedom.

The Bridge from Mindset to Income

Mindset alone does not create income. Income alone does not transform mindset.

The real change happens in the bridge between the two.

Many people get stuck on one side of this bridge. Some work endlessly on mindset—beliefs, affirmations, healing—yet see little financial improvement. Others chase income aggressively—side hustles, strategies, opportunities—without addressing internal patterns, and find themselves exhausted, inconsistent, or unable to sustain gains.

The bridge exists because mindset influences behavior, and behavior influences income. Without behavior, the mindset remains theoretical. Without a mindset, behavior collapses under pressure.

This chapter concept explains how inner clarity becomes outer results in a grounded, step-by-step way.

The bridge begins with perception. Mindset shapes how opportunities are seen. Two people can encounter the same situation—an idea, a skill, a market—and respond differently. One notices a possibility. The other notices risk. This difference is not intelligence; it is internal conditioning. A stable mindset does not guarantee success, but it expands what the mind considers *possible enough to try*. When the mindset shifts from scarcity to realism, perception widens. Options that once felt invisible or threatening become approachable. This is the first plank of the bridge.

The next plank is decision-making. Mindset influences how decisions are made under uncertainty. Income growth always involves uncertainty—time investment, learning curves, and delayed reward. A fragile mindset seeks certainty before acting, often leading to stalls. A grounded mindset accepts uncertainty and acts with structure rather than fear.

This does not mean reckless risk-taking. It means thoughtful movement despite discomfort. Income grows where decisions are made consistently, not where certainty is demanded.

The next critical plank is behavioral consistency. This is where many people fall off the bridge. Even with insight and good decisions, inconsistent behavior breaks momentum. Mindset determines whether a person returns after setbacks or retreats into avoidance. A stable mindset reframes mistakes as data rather than proof of failure.

Income responds to consistency—skills compound. Relationships deepen. Systems improve. Without consistency, income remains unpredictable. This is why mindset work must translate into habits—not inspiration.

Another essential plank is the capacity to delay reward. Most income growth does not pay immediately. It pays later—after learning, practice, and persistence. A mindset shaped by scarcity or urgency struggles here. It seeks fast relief. It abandons paths that do not reward quickly.

A grounded mindset tolerates the gap between effort and outcome. That tolerance allows income to mature rather than collapse prematurely.

The bridge also includes emotional regulation during growth. An income increase brings pressure—expectations, comparisons, fear of loss. Without emotional regulation, progress triggers self-sabotage. A person may stop showing up, overspend, or abandon systems just as momentum builds.

Mindset work creates emotional steadiness. That steadiness allows income to rise without triggering collapse. This is a crucial but rarely discussed connection.

Another plank is identity alignment. Income grows when behavior aligns with identity. A person who sees themselves as capable of learning, improving, and stewarding resources behaves differently from someone who considers income as accidental or undeserved. Identity determines whether income feels natural or threatening.

When identity shifts, income strategies stop feeling like performance and start feeling like expression. This makes the effort sustainable.

The final plank of the bridge is the structure. Income does not flow into chaos. It flows into systems. Mindset prepares the person to build and maintain those systems—tracking, planning, boundaries, reinvestment. Without structure, income leaks. With structure, it accumulates.

This is why mindset without structure produces frustration, and structure without mindset produces burnout. The bridge requires both.

The bridge from mindset to income is not crossed once. It is struck repeatedly. Each income level requires renewed alignment among belief, behavior, and structure. What worked at one level may strain at the next. This is normal. Growth requires recalibration.

This concept helps the reader understand that they are not failing because the mindset "didn't work" or because income strategies "didn't work." They may simply have been standing on one side of the bridge, expecting results to appear on the other.

Mindset prepares the ground. Behavior builds the bridge. Structure allows income to cross and stay.

When all three work together, income stops feeling accidental or exhausting. It results from alignment rather than struggle.

This chapter closes Book 1 by making one truth clear: You do not need to choose between inner work and practical action. Income grows where the two meet.

Book 2 will begin on the other side of this bridge—not with motivation, but with methods that now have somewhere stable to land.

Because mindset alone inspires, income alone stresses. But alignment creates momentum—and momentum creates sustainable wealth.

What "Financial Readiness" Truly Means

Financial readiness is one of the most misunderstood concepts in personal finance. It is often mistaken for wealth, high income, or the absence of struggle. In reality, financial readiness has very little to do with how much money you currently have. It has everything to do with how prepared your life, mindset, and systems are to hold and grow money without breaking down.

Financial readiness is not a destination. It is a condition.

A person is financially ready when money can enter their life without immediately creating chaos—emotionally, mentally, relationally, or structurally. Readiness determines whether money becomes a stabilizing or destabilizing force. At its core, financial readiness means capacity.

Capacity is the ability to:

- Make decisions without panic
- Manage responsibility without resentment
- Handle growth without self-sabotage
- Sustain progress without burnout

Without capacity, money does not improve life—it exposes strain.

One of the clearest indicators of financial readiness is emotional steadiness around money. A financially ready person does not need money to feel okay, nor do they fall apart when money is imperfect. They can engage honestly with their finances—even when things are tight—without avoidance, shame, or emotional overwhelm. This steadiness allows clear thinking, which is essential for good financial decisions.

Financial readiness also means clarity over confusion. The person generally knows where they stand financially. They may not track every detail, but nothing feels completely invisible. They are not guessing mindlessly. They review, reflect, and adjust. This clarity reduces anxiety and increases agency.

Another key aspect of readiness is consistency. A financially ready person does not rely on bursts of motivation or extreme discipline. They have habits they can maintain—small, repeatable actions that support stability. They follow through more often than not. This consistency builds self-trust, which is far more important than temporary effort.

Financial readiness also includes alignment between lifestyle and reality. The person no longer tries to live a life that their current capacity cannot support. They make choices that fit their income, energy, and responsibilities. This honesty protects progress and prevents a constant financial recovery mode.

Importantly, readiness involves a healthy relationship with responsibility. The financially ready person does not avoid responsibility, nor do they carry it as a burden. They understand what is within their control and act there calmly. Responsibility feels like agency, not punishment. This mindset allows growth without fear.

Another defining feature of financial readiness is structure. Money needs systems—however simple—to stay organized. A ready person has some form of structure in place: awareness systems, review habits, basic planning, spending boundaries, and obligations. These structures are flexible, not rigid, but they exist. Money has somewhere to land.

Financial readiness also means identity stability. Money is no longer tied to self-worth, validation, or comparison. Success does not inflate ego. Struggle does not collapse identity. This separation allows money to be handled objectively. Decisions become cleaner. Progress becomes sustainable.

Perhaps one of the most important truths about financial readiness is this: readiness often arrives before visible success.

Many people believe they must wait until their finances improve to feel ready. In reality, readiness is what *allows* finances to improve. It shows up as calm engagement, enhanced habits, clearer boundaries, and reduced self-sabotage long before income changes dramatically.

Financial readiness is also marked by patience with growth. The person understands that stability compounds. They stop rushing, comparing, or forcing outcomes. This patience does not slow progress—it stabilizes it. Rushed growth collapses. Prepared growth lasts.

Another subtle but powerful sign of readiness is the ability to let gains settle. When things improve slightly, the financially ready person does not immediately undo the progress through impulse, fear, or pressure. They allow improvement to become normal. This tolerance for stability is a major indicator of readiness.

Ultimately, financial readiness means this: You are no longer waiting for money to save you. You are preparing to manage money well when it arrives.

It means you can receive more without losing peace. You can earn more without burning out. You can grow without self-betrayal.

Financial readiness is not loud. It does not feel like confidence or excitement. It feels like:

- Calm responsibility
- Quiet consistency
- Clear awareness
- Steady self-trust

And this is why financial readiness is the true foundation of economic freedom.

Money flows where it is respected. Growth settles where it is supported. And readiness is what makes both possible.

This understanding completes Book 1's purpose: to transform the reader from someone chasing money into someone capable of holding it well.

From this place, income strategies finally work—not because the world changed, but because the person did.

Emotional Stability and Money

Money is not just a financial tool. It is an emotional trigger.

For many people, money activates fear, urgency, hope, shame, pressure, comparison, or a need for control. These emotions often operate beneath awareness, quietly influencing decisions long before logic has a chance to intervene. This is why two people with the same income and knowledge can experience vastly different financial outcomes.

The difference is often emotional stability.

Emotional stability around money does not mean the absence of emotion. It means the ability to feel without being driven. It is the capacity to experience stress, desire, disappointment, or excitement without allowing those feelings to hijack decisions. This capacity is foundational to financial maturity.

When emotional stability is low, money decisions become reactive. Spending happens to relieve discomfort. Avoidance happens to escape anxiety. Risk-taking happens to feel powerful. Over-saving happens to feel safe. None of these behaviors is inherently wrong—but when they are driven primarily by emotion rather than intention, they create instability.

One of the most common emotional patterns around money is fear-based decision-making. Fear can show up as scarcity—worry that money will run out—or as loss aversion—panic at the idea of making the "wrong" choice. Fear narrows thinking. It pushes people toward short-term relief rather than long-term stability. Decisions are made quickly, defensively, and often regretfully.

Emotional stability allows fear to be felt without being obeyed. The person can acknowledge uncertainty and still act thoughtfully.

Another major emotional influence is shame. Shame tells a person they are bad, broken, or behind because of their financial situation. When shame is present, engagement disappears. People avoid looking at their finances, asking questions, or planning for the future. Avoidance then worsens the situation, reinforcing the shame cycle.

Emotional stability interrupts this loop. It replaces self-judgment with observation. Money becomes something to manage, not something to hide from.

Excitement and urgency are also emotionally destabilizing. Sudden opportunities, income spikes, or financial wins can trigger impulsive decisions—overspending, overcommitting, or abandoning systems. Without emotional stability, progress creates as much risk as struggle. This is why many people lose money not during hardship, but during improvement.

Stability allows gains to settle. It supports restraint without deprivation and enjoyment without collapse.

Another critical emotional factor is attachment to identity. When money is tied to self-worth, validation, or comparison, emotions spike with every financial change. Wins inflate ego. Losses feel personal. This volatility makes consistent decision-making nearly impossible. Emotional stability requires separating money from identity so that decisions can be made calmly and objectively.

Emotional stability also affects patience. Most financial growth requires delayed gratification. Without emotional regulation, waiting feels intolerable. The person abandons paths that do not pay quickly or demands results before systems mature. Stability allows a person to stay the course through uncertainty and slow progress.

Importantly, emotional instability around money is not a character flaw. It is often the result of past experiences—financial stress, unpredictability, pressure, or learned scarcity. The nervous system learned to associate money with threat or relief—emotional reactions developed as survival responses, not failures.

This is why discipline alone cannot fix money problems. Without emotional stability, discipline feels like punishment and eventually collapses. Stability creates the emotional safety that allows discipline to function.

Emotional stability with money looks like:

- Being able to review finances without spiraling
- Making decisions without rushing or freezing
- Tolerating uncertainty without panic
- Allowing progress without self-sabotage
- Recovering from mistakes without self-attack

It does not require constant calm. It requires recovery. The ability to return to clarity after emotional activation is what matters most.

As emotional stability grows, money decisions become steadier. Patterns shift naturally. Avoidance decreases. Impulses soften. The relationship with money becomes less dramatic and more practical.

This is why emotional stability is not separate from financial readiness—it *is* financial readiness.

Money does not require perfection. It requires presence.

And presence is only possible when emotions are regulated rather than suppressed or indulged.

When emotional stability is present:

- Money becomes information, not judgment
- Decisions become intentional, not reactive
- Growth becomes sustainable, not fragile

Ultimately, emotional stability allows money to take its proper place—not as a source of fear or validation, but as a tool that supports life rather than controls it.

This concept completes the inner foundation of financial readiness. From here, income can grow without destabilizing identity, peace, or progress—because the emotional system holding it is finally strong enough to do so.

Aligning Habits, Values, and Goals

Many people set goals. Many people hold strong values. Many people practice daily habits.

Yet progress still feels slow, inconsistent, or exhausting.

The missing link is often alignment.

Alignment means that what you do repeatedly (habits), what matters most to you (values), and what you are aiming toward (goals) are pointing in the same direction. When they are aligned, progress feels steady and sustainable. When they are misaligned, effort increases, but results stall.

Misalignment does not always look like failure. Often, it seems like constant effort without lasting change.

Values are the *why*. Goals are the *what*. Habits are the *how*.

When any one of these operates in isolation, tension forms. Many people say they value stability, peace, or freedom, but their daily habits are reactive, impulsive, or disorganized. Others set ambitious financial goals, but their habits are not built to support them. Some hold strong values but never translate them into concrete goals. The result is frustration—not because the person lacks discipline, but because their system is internally conflicted.

Alignment begins with value clarity. Values are not ideals you admire; they are principles you are willing to organize your life around. If stability is a true value, then consistency, structure, and patience must be honored in daily behavior. If freedom is a value, then habits that reduce dependency and chaos must be prioritized. When values are vague, habits drift. When values are clear, habits gain direction.

Goals translate values into outcomes. A goal is not just something you want—it is a value made specific. For example, valuing security might translate into a goal of building an emergency fund. Valuing growth might mean investing in skill development or diversifying income sources. Goals give values a timeline and a form.

Habits are where alignment becomes visible. Habits reveal what is actually being honored. You do not live your values in theory—you live them in repetition. If habits contradict stated values, the body experiences internal friction. That friction drains energy and creates self-doubt. For example, if a person values long-term stability but consistently makes short-term emotional decisions, they experience guilt and frustration. Not because they are weak—but because their habits are undermining what they care about.

Alignment removes this friction.

When habits support goals, and goals express values, effort feels lighter. Decisions feel clearer. Follow-through improves—not through pressure, but through coherence.

Another critical aspect of alignment is realism. Many people choose goals that reflect comparison rather than capacity. They want outcomes that their current habits cannot sustain. This creates constant self-criticism. True alignment respects current reality while gently expanding it. Goals are challenging but achievable. Habits are small enough to repeat. Values remain steady.

Alignment also requires prioritization. You cannot optimize every value at once. There are seasons where stability matters more than speed, or learning matters more than earning. Alignment means choosing which values lead right now and adjusting habits accordingly. This prevents burnout and scattered effort.

In finances, alignment often looks like this:

- **Values:** stability, peace, independence
- **Goals:** consistent saving, reduced debt, predictable cash flow
- **Habits:** regular review, modest saving, thoughtful spending

When these align, money stops feeling chaotic. Progress compounds naturally.

Another powerful effect of alignment is identity reinforcement. When habits, values, and goals match, the mind updates identity: *This is who I am now.* Identity then supports behavior, reducing the need for constant motivation.

Misalignment keeps identity conflicted. Alignment stabilizes it.

Alignment also protects against self-sabotage. When progress begins, aligned systems allow it to settle. There is no internal conflict pulling behavior in opposite directions. Growth feels safe because it aligns with values, and habits are ready to support it.

Importantly, alignment is not static. As life changes, alignment must be reviewed. Values deepen. Goals evolve. Habits adjust. This is not instability—it is maturity. Regular reflection keeps alignment alive.

Aligning habits, values, and goals does not require dramatic change. It requires honesty and intention. Small shifts create large effects when alignment is present.

When alignment exists:

- Decisions feel simpler
- Discipline feels protective
- Progress feels earned
- Stability feels natural

You stop fighting yourself. You stop forcing outcomes. You start moving as one system.

Ultimately, alignment is what turns effort into momentum. Values give meaning. Goals give direction. Habits give power.

When all three work together, financial readiness is no longer something you pursue—it becomes something you embody.

What Changes After This Foundation Is Laid

When the foundation described in this book is truly laid, life does not suddenly become perfect. There is no dramatic overnight transformation, no instant wealth, and no disappearance of challenges. What changes is something far more important and far more permanent: the way you move through decisions, pressure, and opportunity.

The first and most noticeable change is internal stability. Money no longer dominates your emotional state. You are not calm because everything is ideal—you are relaxed because you understand how to respond. Financial situations that once triggered panic, avoidance, or impulsive action now meet a steadier version of you. This stability is not confidence built on outcomes; it is confidence built on capacity.

Another profound change is clarity of direction. Before the foundation, effort may have felt scattered—trying many things, reacting to pressure, chasing relief. After the foundation, your actions feel more deliberate. You know what matters right now. You understand your season. You stop forcing progress and start building it intentionally. Even when results are slow, your direction feels right.

Decision-making also changes. Decisions become less emotional and more grounded. You still feel desire, fear, and uncertainty—but they no longer control you. You pause. You evaluate. You choose. This pause alone prevents countless financial mistakes. You begin to notice how often past problems were not caused by lack of opportunity, but by rushed or emotionally driven decisions.

Another key shift is reduced self-sabotage. When things improve—even slightly—you no longer feel the urge to undo progress. Stability stops feeling suspicious. You allow gains to settle. You stop spending to relieve pressure or prove worth. This ability to tolerate improvement is one of the clearest signs that the foundation has taken hold.

Your relationship with discipline also transforms. Discipline no longer feels like something imposed on you. It feels like something you use to protect what you are building. Boundaries feel supportive instead of restrictive.

Consistency feels natural instead of exhausting. You stop swinging between extremes and begin moving steadily.

Money itself begins to behave differently. Not because it has changed—but because you have changed. Leaks become visible. Systems strengthen. Awareness replaces avoidance. Even without a dramatic income increase, money starts to stay longer. When income does grow, it integrates instead of overwhelming.

Another important change is identity stabilization. You no longer see yourself as "bad with money" or "behind." You see yourself as someone in progress, capable of learning and managing responsibility. This identity shift removes shame and comparison. You stop measuring yourself against others and start measuring alignment with your own values.

Relationships often shift as well. Clearer boundaries emerge. You become more honest about what you can and cannot support. You stop using money to compensate for guilt, fear, or obligation. This may feel uncomfortable at first, but it creates healthier dynamics and preserves both finances and peace.

You also become more selective. Opportunities are no longer chased out of desperation. You evaluate them based on fit, sustainability, and alignment. This discernment prevents burnout and protects momentum. You begin to understand that saying no is often what allows the right yes to arrive.

Perhaps most importantly, your timeline changes. You stop rushing. You stop trying to "catch up." You respect the process of growth. This patience does not slow you down—it prevents collapse. Prepared growth compounds. Rushed growth breaks.

After this foundation is laid, effort becomes more effective—learning sticks. Habits hold. Progress compounds quietly. You may still face challenges, but you no longer face them as someone who hopes money will save you. You face them as someone who can respond.

This foundation does not make life easy. It makes life manageable.

And manageability is what allows expansion.

Once this foundation exists, income strategies finally work—not because they are new, but because they now have somewhere stable to land. Book 2 will build on this reality. It will focus on earning, opportunity, and strategy—but without needing to heal what should already be solid.

This is the shift: You stop chasing money to fix instability. You start building money on top of stability.

That is what changes. And once it changes, it does not go back.

The foundation you have built here becomes the quiet strength behind every future financial decision—ensuring that growth, when it comes, stays.

Preparing for Book 2: Learning How to Make Money

Book 1 was never meant to teach you how to make money. It was meant to prepare you to handle money well once you start making it.

This distinction is critical because most financial frustration does not come from a lack of opportunity—it comes from a lack of readiness. People often rush into income strategies before their inner systems are stable. When that happens, money is earned but not held, progress begins but does not last, and effort increases without proportional reward.

Book 1 was about building the *container.*

Book 2 is about filling it.

Before learning how to make money, several things needed to be addressed:

- Emotional instability around money
- Scarcity-based decision-making
- Weak structures and financial leaks
- Lack of consistency and self-trust
- Confusion between identity, worth, and income

Without resolving these, income strategies would either overwhelm you or collapse under pressure.

Now, that groundwork is laid.

Preparing for Book 2 means recognizing a shift in *who you are becoming*. You are no longer approaching money from desperation, fantasy, or avoidance. You are approaching it from the perspectives of capacity, clarity, and readiness.

This matters because making money is not just about tactics—it is about execution under uncertainty.

Every income path involves:

- Learning curves
- Delayed results
- Inconsistent early returns
- Mistakes and recalibration
- Discipline without immediate reward

Only a person with emotional stability, realistic expectations, and consistent habits can navigate this phase without quitting prematurely or self-sabotaging their progress.

That is why Book 1 came first.

Book 2 will focus on *practical income creation*—but not hype-driven hustles or unrealistic shortcuts. It will teach how money is actually made in modern conditions, with an emphasis on sustainability, skill leverage, and ethical growth.

Book 2 assumes that:

- You can follow through without perfection
- You can sit with uncertainty without panic
- You can manage small wins without undoing them
- You can delay gratification without resentment
- You can build steadily instead of chasing fast relief

These are not assumptions about intelligence or talent. They are assumptions about readiness.

Book 2 will explore:

- How value is created and exchanged
- How skills become income
- How to identify viable income paths
- How to start small and scale responsibly
- How to avoid common income traps
- How to align earnings with values and capacity

It will not try to "motivate" you. It will equip you.

Because motivation fades. Preparation lasts.

Preparing for Book 2 also means releasing one final illusion: that making money will fix inner instability.

Money magnifies systems. You have built better ones.

Now, money can become a tool rather than a test.

The transition from Book 1 to Book 2 is not about urgency. It is about an opportunity to attend a readiness meeting.

You are no longer asking: "How do I escape financial struggle?"

You are now asking: "How do I build income in a way I can sustain?"

That question signals maturity.

Book 2 does not promise ease. It promises clarity, realism, and direction.

And because the foundation is now solid, what you build next will not collapse under its own weight.

You are no longer preparing to chase money. You are deliberately preparing to create it.

That is the shift.

And that is why Book 2 can finally begin.

BONUS SECTION

FOUNDATION TOOLS

This bonus section exists for one reason: to help you live what you've learned.

Insight without application fades. Understanding without tools stays theoretical.

The tools in this section are not complicated, rigid, or overwhelming. They are intentionally simple—because simplicity is what survives stress, emotion, and real life.

You do not need to use every tool at once. You only need to return to them consistently.

Tool 1: The Financial Awareness Check-In (10 Minutes)

This is your core tool.

Not a budget. Not a spreadsheet marathon. Just awareness.

Once a week (or every two weeks), ask yourself:

- Where did my money generally go?
- What felt aligned?
- What felt draining or reactive?
- Did I avoid anything?
- What do I want to adjust next week?

You are not fixing everything. You are noticing patterns.

Awareness is the foundation of all financial maturity. Nothing changes that is not seen.

Tool 2: The Emotional Money Pause

Before a financial decision that feels urgent or emotional, pause and ask:

- What am I feeling right now?
- What problem do I think this money will solve?
- Will this decision still feel right tomorrow?

You do not need a perfect answer. You only need to interrupt the automatic reaction.

This pause alone prevents many mistakes—not because you become stricter, but because you become present.

Tool 3: The Small Stewardship Practice

Choose a small amount of money and manage it intentionally. It could be:

- A fixed weekly savings amount
- A specific category you track carefully
- A modest emergency buffer
- A small reinvestment fund

The size does not matter. The care does.

This practice builds self-trust and readiness. Large responsibility grows from small stewardship.

Tool 4: The Identity Reframe Statement

When old financial narratives appear, replace identity language with process language. Instead of:

- "I'm bad with money," says:
- "I'm learning to manage money with consistency."

Instead of:

- "I always mess this up," says:
- "I'm adjusting my system."

This is not positive thinking. It is accurate thinking.

Identity shapes behavior. Reframe identity, and behavior follows.

Tool 5: The Leak Review

Once a month, review gently:

- Where does money leave quietly?
- What expenses repeat automatically?
- What costs exist because of urgency or avoidance?

You are not hunting yourself. You are sealing gaps. Most financial progress comes from reducing leaks, not increasing income.

Tool 6: The Readiness Compass

When evaluating any new opportunity, ask:

- Does this match my current capacity?
- Can I sustain this without burnout?
- Does this support stability or create chaos?
- Am I choosing from clarity or pressure?

If an opportunity demands more chaos than growth, it is not aligned—no matter how attractive it looks.

Readiness protects momentum.

Tool 7: The Consistency Rule

Never try to do everything. Always try to do something repeatable.

- Small savings beat aggressive savings once
- Gentle tracking beats perfect tracking briefly
- Returning beats quitting

Consistency builds identity. Identity sustains wealth.

Tool 8: The Foundation Reset

When you feel overwhelmed, return to this order:

1. Calm your emotions
2. Review awareness (not numbers alone)
3. Re-establish structure
4. Take one small aligned action

You do not need to start over. You only need to return to the foundation.

How to Use This Bonus Section

- Bookmark it
- Return when confused
- Revisit during growth
- Use it when things improve (most important)

This section is not only for emergencies. It is for maintenance and maturity.

Final Reminder

You are no longer building habits to "fix" yourself. You are building systems to support who you are becoming.

These tools are not here to control you. They are here to protect your progress.

With this foundation in place, Book 2 will not overwhelm you. It will activate you.

You are no longer preparing to survive on money. You are preparing to create it responsibly.

And now, you have the tools to do so.

Financial Belief Self-Assessment

This self-assessment helps you identify the beliefs quietly shaping your financial behavior—often without your awareness. Answer honestly. Do not answer based on who you *want* to be. Answer based on how you *actually think and feel* most of the time.

You may notice discomfort. That is awareness forming—not failure.

How to Use This Assessment

- Read each statement slowly
- Rate how true it feels for you right now
- Use this scale:

1 — Strongly disagree

2 — Disagree

3 — Neutral / unsure

4 — Agree

5 — Strongly agree

Write your number beside each statement.

Section 1: Money & Identity

1. My financial situation says something about my worth as a person
2. I feel behind compared to others financially
3. I often judge myself harshly for money mistakes
4. I believe some people are just naturally good with money, and I am not
5. When money improves, I feel pressure to prove myself

Section 2: Scarcity & Safety

6. I worry that money will disappear quickly
7. I feel anxious looking at my finances
8. Saving feels difficult because emergencies always come up
9. I often feel one step away from financial trouble
10. Stability feels unfamiliar or temporary

Section 3: Control & Avoidance

11. I avoid tracking money because it stresses me out
12. I feel overwhelmed by financial decisions
13. I delay dealing with money issues until they become urgent
14. I go through cycles of being very strict, then giving up
15. I feel guilty when I spend money on myself

Section 4: Growth & Responsibility

16. More money feels like more pressure, not more freedom
17. I fear failing if I try something new financially
18. I struggle to follow through consistently
19. Discipline feels restrictive rather than supportive
20. Responsibility around money feels heavy

Section 5: Readiness & Capacity

21. I can look at my finances calmly, even when they are imperfect
22. I trust myself to make better financial decisions than before
23. I feel capable of managing more money responsibly
24. I believe financial skills can be learned
25. I am becoming more consistent than reactive

Scoring & Reflection

You do not need a total score. Instead, look for patterns.

If you scored mostly 4s and 5s in Sections 1–4

This indicates active limiting beliefs around money, safety, and self-trust. This does not mean you are unready—it means you are becoming *aware*. Awareness is the first real shift.

If you scored mostly 1s and 2s in Sections 1–4

This suggests emotional distance from money struggles may already be forming. Readiness is emerging.

If you scored mostly 4s and 5s in Section 5

This is a strong sign of financial readiness in formation. Your internal systems are stabilizing.

Mixed scores

This is the most common—and healthiest—result. It means old beliefs are loosening, but not fully released yet.

Key Reflection Questions

Take time with these. Write if possible.

- Which statements triggered discomfort?
- Which felt familiar?
- Which surprised you?
- Which beliefs feel inherited rather than chosen?
- What belief do you feel ready to outgrow?

Reframing Exercise (Optional but Powerful)

Choose one statement you rated 4 or 5 and rewrite it using grounded truth.

Example:

Original belief: "I'm bad with money."

Reframed truth: "I am learning to manage money with awareness and consistency."

This is not pretending. It is updating.

Why This Assessment Matters

Beliefs shape:

- Decisions

- Habits
- Emotional reactions
- Financial outcomes

What you see, you can change. What stays hidden, stays in control.

This assessment is not meant to make you feel behind. It is intended to show you how far you've already come.

Important Reminder

Financial belief change is not instant. It is layered.

You do not replace beliefs by force. You replace them with practice, awareness, and consistency.

This assessment marks the moment you stop guessing and start choosing what you believe about money.

Scarcity-to-Stability Reflection Prompts

Scarcity is not just about money. It is about how the mind responds to uncertainty.

These prompts help you notice where scarcity still lives—and where stability is already forming.

Section 1: Recognizing Scarcity Patterns

1. When I think about money, what is the first emotion that appears?

2. What situations make me feel rushed, pressured, or panicked financially?
3. What money thoughts repeat most often when I'm stressed?
4. Where do I feel "behind" even when I am making progress?
5. What financial situations do I tend to avoid?

Reflection note: Scarcity often shows up as urgency, fear, or avoidance—not logic.

Section 2: Understanding the Origin

6. What early experiences shaped how I see money?
7. What messages about money did I hear growing up?
8. When did I first learn to worry about money?
9. What financial patterns did I observe in the people around me?
10. Which beliefs feel inherited rather than chosen?

Reflection note: Scarcity is learned. What is learned can be unlearned.

Section 3: Noticing Survival Mode Thinking

11. When I make financial decisions, am I usually reacting or choosing?
12. Do I prioritize short-term relief over long-term stability?

13. How do I respond emotionally when money improves?
14. Do I feel unsafe when things are calm?
15. What does "enough" feel like to me?

Reflection note: Survival mode prepares for threat—even when none is present.

Section 4: Identifying Stability Signals

16. When have I handled money calmly, even under pressure?
17. What financial habits feel supportive rather than stressful?
18. Where have I shown consistency instead of intensity?
19. What financial decisions am I proud of—even small ones?
20. What does stability currently look like in my life?

Reflection note: Stability is often quietly forming.

Section 5: Releasing Scarcity Narratives

21. What beliefs no longer match my current capacity?
22. What fear am I ready to outgrow?
23. What story about money am I tired of repeating?
24. What would change if I stopped seeing money as an emergency?
25. What belief feels safer to adopt now?

Reflection note: You do not need to erase scarcity—only loosen its grip.

Section 6: Choosing Stability Intentionally

26. What does financial stability mean *to me*, not society?
27. What small habit supports that version of stability?
28. How can I respond more slowly to financial decisions?
29. What boundary would protect my peace?
30. What does my future self need from me now?

Reflection note: Stability grows through intention, not pressure.

Optional Closing Exercise: The Stability Anchor

Complete this sentence slowly: "When I feel financial pressure, I choose to respond with __________ instead of __________."

Repeat it when urgency appears.

Final Reminder

Scarcity does not disappear because money increases. It disappears because capacity increases.

Every calm choice you make is a vote for stability. Every pause replaces urgency with wisdom.

You are not moving from a state of lack to one of abundance. You are moving from fear to steadiness. And steadiness is what allows everything else to grow.

14-Day Financial Reset Guide

A foundation-first reset for clarity, calm, and consistency

How to Use This Reset

- Spend 10–20 minutes per day
- Do not try to "fix everything."
- If you miss a day, continue—do not restart
- The goal is stability, not intensity

DAY 1 — Pause & Reset Your Nervous System

Focus: Calm before control

- Take 3 slow breaths
- Remind yourself: *"Nothing is wrong. I am resetting."*
- Write one sentence: *"Right now, money feels ___________."*

Why this matters: Financial clarity cannot form in panic.

DAY 2 — Observe Without Judgment

Focus: Awareness

- Review your last 7–14 days of spending

- Do not categorize or analyze yet
- Just notice patterns

Write:

- What surprised me?
- What felt automatic?

DAY 3 — Name Emotional Triggers

Focus: Emotional awareness

Answer:

- When do I spend impulsively?
- When do I avoid money?
- What emotions show up most often?

Awareness weakens emotional control.

DAY 4 — Identify One Financial Leak

Focus: Containment

Choose one recurring expense or habit that quietly drains money.

Ask:

- Does this support my stability?
- Can I reduce or pause it?

Do not eliminate everything.

DAY 5 — Define Your Version of Stability

Focus: Values clarity

Complete: "Financial stability means __________ to me."

This becomes your compass.

DAY 6 — Create One Simple Rule

Focus: Gentle structure

Examples:

- Pause 24 hours before non-essential purchases
- Review finances weekly
- Save a small fixed amount

One rule. Not many.

DAY 7 — Mid-Reset Check-In

Focus: Reflection

Ask:

- What feels lighter?
- What feels resistant?
- What am I learning about myself?

You are not behind—you are forming clarity.

DAY 8 — Practice Small Stewardship

Focus: Readiness

Choose a small amount to manage intentionally (even very small).

This builds trust—not wealth yet.

DAY 9 — Replace One Limiting Belief

Focus: Identity update

Write one belief you are ready to outgrow.

Example: "Money never stays."

Replace with: "Money stays where there is structure."

DAY 10 — Set a Gentle Boundary

Focus: Protection

Choose one boundary:

- Spending
- Supporting others
- Over-committing
- Emotional buying

Boundaries protect progress.

DAY 11 — Create an Awareness System

Focus: Sustainability

Decide:

- When will I review money? (weekly/bi-weekly)
- How long? (10–15 minutes)

No rigid budgets—just visibility.

DAY 12 — Practice Emotional Pause

Focus: Regulation

Before spending today, pause and ask:

- What am I feeling?
- Will this decision support stability?

Pause changes outcomes.

DAY 13 — Acknowledge Progress

Focus: Reinforcement

Write 3 things you are doing better—even if small.

Stability grows through recognition.

DAY 14 — Declare Readiness

Focus: Integration

Complete this sentence: "I am becoming financially ready because __________."

This is not confidence. It is capacity awareness.

After the 14 Days

You are not "done." You are reset.

What has changed:

- Less panic
- More clarity
- Better awareness
- Stronger self-trust

This is the foundation that allows income growth to last.

Important Reminder

Do not rush to do more. Let this reset settle.

Stability must be *lived*, not forced.

RETURN HERE IF YOU FEEL STUCK

Feeling stuck does not mean you are failing. It usually means you are between an old way of operating and a new one.

This page is not here to push you forward. It is here to help you regain your footing.

Take a breath. Read slowly.

If You Feel Overwhelmed

Stop trying to solve everything.

You are not meant to hold your entire financial future in your head at once.

Right now, do only this:

- Pause
- Breathe
- Reduce the problem to *one next step*

Ask yourself: "What is the smallest stabilizing action I can take today?"

Small actions restore momentum. Big pressure destroys it.

If You Feel Discouraged

Discouragement often appears when effort is present, but results are slow.

This does not mean nothing is happening.

It means change is integrating beneath the surface.

Ask yourself:

- What am I doing differently than before?
- Where am I more aware?
- Where am I less reactive?

Progress often shows up as *calm* rather than excitement.

If You Feel Like Giving Up

Before quitting, check this: Are you tired — or are you truly done?

Most quitting happens because of exhaustion, not clarity.

If you are tired:

- Rest
- Simplify
- Reduce expectations
- Return to basics

You do not need a new plan. You need recovery, not retreat.

If You Feel Behind

There is no universal financial timeline.

Comparison creates urgency. Urgency destroys wisdom.

You are not behind—you are on a different sequence.

Ask: "Am I more prepared today than I was before?"

Preparation is progress.

If You Feel Confused

Confusion is often a sign of too much information, not too little clarity. Do not add more input.

Instead:

- Remove noise
- Return to what you know
- Focus on what you can control today

Clarity returns when noise reduces.

If Money Feels Heavy Again

This happens. Old emotional patterns do not disappear instantly. They resurface under stress.

This is not regression. It is practice.

When money feels heavy:

- Slow down decisions
- Avoid urgency-based choices
- Return to awareness, not control

Stability returns through gentleness, not force.

If You Feel Like You've "Lost Progress"

You have not lost what you have learned.

Skills do not disappear. Awareness does not vanish. You may feel disconnected—but the foundation remains.

Return to:

- Consistency over intensity
- Order before expansion
- Care for small things

These principles do not expire.

The One-Page Reset

If everything feels scattered, do this:

1. Calm your emotions
2. Look at your finances briefly (no judgment)

3. Identify one small adjustment
4. Take that action
5. Stop for the day

Momentum returns through completion, not pressure.

Read This Slowly

You are not broken. You are not late. You are not failing. You are learning how to become someone who can hold stability.

That takes time. That takes repetition. That takes patience.

When You're Ready to Move Again

Do not rush.

Return to:

- Awareness
- Small stewardship
- Consistency
- Calm decisions

Forward motion will follow naturally.

Final Reminder

You do not need to restart. You do not need to punish yourself. You do not need to "do better."

You only need to return.

Return to what you know. Return to the foundation. Return to yourself. This page will always be here.

Book Teaser

You are no longer trying to fix your relationship with money. You are ready to deliberately create it.

Book 2 begins where most books rush too early—income creation—but with a critical difference: this time, you are prepared to sustain what you build.

This next phase is not about chasing quick wins or unrealistic hustles. It is about understanding how money is made in real life, how value becomes income, and how to grow earnings without chaos, burnout, or self-sabotage. You will learn how to:

- Turn skills into income
- Identify realistic earning paths
- Start small and build steadily
- Avoid income traps and false promises
- Grow money in ways your life can actually hold

Book 1 helped you become ready.

Book 2 will help you become capable.

Not overnight. Not recklessly. But intentionally, sustainably, and with clarity.

You are no longer asking, *"How do I survive financially?"*

You are now asking, *"How do I build income that lasts?"*

That question changes everything.

Book 2 is where the work begins.

About the Author

ADURA GBEMI ADEGBOYE is a writer, educator, and reflective thinker focused on the inner foundations that shape financial stability, personal discipline, and long-term growth.

With a deep interest in the psychology of money, emotional awareness, and life principles, Adura's work explores why financial progress often collapses when inner readiness is overlooked. Rather than promoting shortcuts or hustle culture, his writing emphasizes preparation, clarity, responsibility, and sustainable systems that sustain growth.

Adura's approach is grounded, practical, and human. He believes that money is not merely a financial tool, but a mirror that reveals habits, beliefs, and emotional patterns. Through his work, he helps readers move from scarcity and confusion to steadiness and self-trust—before pursuing income or wealth.

Before the Money Comes reflects his commitment to helping individuals build the inner structure required to hold financial progress without chaos, burnout, or self-sabotage.

Adura Gbemi Adegboye writes for readers who are ready to slow down, prepare wisely, and build a life—and finances—that can stand.

Acknowledgments

This book was not written in isolation.

It is the result of reflection, observation, unlearning, and quiet rebuilding—shaped by experiences, conversations, and moments that challenged how I understood money, stability, and responsibility.

I acknowledge every person who has struggled financially and still chose to keep learning. Your honesty, resilience, and willingness to question old patterns inspired the heart of this work. This book exists because real people needed something deeper than advice—something steady, human, and grounding.

I am grateful for the voices, books, teachings, and life lessons that emphasized wisdom over urgency, patience over pressure, and preparation over shortcuts. Each insight contributed to the foundation on which this book stands.

To those who supported this work directly or indirectly—through encouragement, honest feedback, or simply believing in the importance of this message—thank you. Your presence mattered more than you may know.

I also acknowledge the reader.

If you are holding this book, it means you were willing to pause, reflect, and prepare rather than rush. That willingness is not small. It is a sign of maturity and courage. Thank you for trusting this process and for allowing this book to meet you where you are.

This work is dedicated to clarity, steadiness, and lasting growth. May it serve you well.

www.ingramcontent.com/pod-product-compliance
Lightning Source LLC
LaVergne TN
LVHW050911210926
848482LV00012B/403